Curriculum Mapping
for **Differentiated Instruction, K-8**

San Diego Christian College
2100 Greenfield Drive
El Cajon, CA 92019

375.001
L271c

25.16
FP

Curriculum Mapping
for Differentiated Instruction, κ-8

Michelle A. Langa
Janice L. Yost

CORWIN PRESS
A SAGE Publications Company
Thousand Oaks, CA 91320

Copyright © 2007 by Corwin Press

All rights reserved. When forms and sample documents are included, their use is authorized only by educators, local school sites, and/or noncommercial or nonprofit entities who have purchased the book. Except for that usage, no part of this book may be reproduced or utilized in any form or by any means, electronic or mechanical, including photocopying, recording, or by any information storage and retrieval system, without permission in writing from the publisher.

For information:

Corwin Press
A Sage Publications Company
2455 Teller Road
Thousand Oaks, California 91320
www.corwinpress.com

Sage Publications Ltd.
1 Oliver's Yard
55 City Road
London EC1Y 1SP
United Kingdom

Sage Publications India Pvt. Ltd.
B-42, Panchsheel Enclave
Post Box 4109
New Delhi 110 017 India

Printed in the United States of America

Library of Congress Cataloging-in-Publication Data

Langa, Michelle A.
Curriculum mapping for differentiated instruction, K–8 / Michelle A. Langa and Janice L. Yost.
    p. cm.
Includes bibliographical references and index.
ISBN 1-4129-1494-9 or 978-1-4129-1494-9 (cloth)
ISBN 1-4129-1495-7 or 978-1-4129-1495-6 (pbk.)
    1. Teacher participation in curriculum planning—United States. 2. Individualized instruction—United States. I. Yost, Janice L. II. Title.
LB2806.15.L36 2007
375'.001—dc22

                                                     2006011902

Printed on acid-free paper

06 07 08 09 10   10 9 8 7 6 5 4 3 2 1

Acquiring Editor:	Faye Zucker
Editorial Assistant:	Gem Rabanera
Production Editor:	Libby Larson
Copy Editor:	Brenda Weight
Typesetter:	C&M Digitals (P) Ltd.
Proofreader:	Sally Scott
Indexer:	Rick Hurd
Cover Designer:	Audrey Snodgrass

Contents

Every teacher in America faces new challenges, namely, assessment and accountability. The momentum for these challenges lies in the emergence of the standards movement, and the passages of the Goals 2000: Educate America Act, the No Child Left Behind Act of 2001, and the reauthorization of IDEA, now called the Individuals with Disabilities Education Improvement Act of 2004. The effects of these factors will be described to help teachers comprehend the critical need to reframe their instructional practices.

Factors that promote successful learning focus on achievement using Bloom's taxonomy, metacognitive strategies, positive expectations, mutually developed norms, student self-assessment, shared leadership, respect for diversity, and inviting physical space.

This chapter provides a brief overview of the development of curriculum mapping. It covers topics such as why teachers should use curriculum maps, the process of curriculum mapping, and the benefits of this approach for teachers, students, and their parents.

List of Figures

Preface

Quite simply, it is extremely difficult for a teacher to synthesize and implement all the existing research-based initiatives. Teachers are constantly asked to develop challenging lessons that maintain the students' interest, address the children's individual learning styles and special needs, make connections among the disciplines, incorporate a variety of modalities and strategies, all while teaching in a heterogeneous/mixed-ability setting, with minimal planning time and limited resources. There hardly seems enough time in a day to accomplish these tasks while taking attendance, reading daily announcements, maintaining classroom control, and, by the way, remaining conversant in educational research!

As former teachers and now staff developers, we have experienced the frustration of wanting to try a different approach but have had little time and few resources to try something new. Six years ago, we decided to change that. Embarking on a long-range plan with the help of school administration and a teacher-led professional development committee, we were able to influence teachers from four school districts to reflect on their teaching. Our collective hope was that teachers would differentiate their lessons according to student needs and learning styles, map their curriculum, and develop interdisciplinary units. To our surprise, we achieved much more than that.

How did this all start? We became intrigued by the wealth of information coming from brain-based and curriculum and instruction research. By drawing on the works of several prominent researchers, such as Armstrong (2000); Arter (2001); Bloom (1956); Carroll (1971); Cooper (2001); Danielson (1996); Gardner (1983, 1999); Jacobs (1997, 2005); Kallick (2005); Marzano (2003); McTighe (1997); Strong, Silver, & Perini (2000, 2001); Stronge (2002); Tomlinson (1999, 2000, 2001); Wiggins (1998); Wolfe (2001); Zull (2002); and others, we were able to create an integrated, teacher-friendly model that makes "common sense" connections.

It is the aim of this book to provide our audience of classroom teachers in grades K–8 with an easy-to-read book based on research, blended approaches, and real-life strategies that work.

Our essential question for this book is *"How can research influence your instructional practices?"* To help you answer that question, we intend to provide a refresher on the history of the standards movement and two recent pieces of legislation, the No Child Left Behind Act and the Individuals with Disabilities Improvement Act. These two major developments have prompted significant changes in instructional practices as well as licensure requirements for teacher certification.

We will review several key factors that assist teachers in creating a student-centered classroom that is focused on achievement. While we realize that there are many factors that must be considered in creating a student-centered environment, we intend to cover only six, namely: creating an environment of respect and rapport, establishing a culture for learning by using metacognition, using Bloom's taxonomy, implementing student self-assessment, organizing physical space, and giving technology a place in your classroom.

We will examine curriculum mapping and its benefits in providing teachers with a clear understanding of a standards-based curriculum and its revitalized relationship to instruction. In addition, we will illustrate how good assessment tools are needed to provide accountability. We will examine rubrics and the parts they play in assisting students to meet higher achievement goals.

Although they are older and well-reviewed theories, we intend to revisit Gardner's multiple intelligences and Strong, Silver, and Perini's learning styles. We believe that, in this new era of accountability, these theories must be incorporated into lesson planning. We will show teachers how to accomplish this in just a few hours with every new unit they plan.

We have also composed a comparison of the major teaching models to support teachers in choosing aspects of each approach that will stretch their instructional repertoire. As lifelong learners, we must continue to grow to prevent becoming entrenched in teaching the same way we have always taught.

Finally, we will demonstrate the central tenet of this book, namely, how combining and applying a student-centered climate, curriculum mapping, using standards and rubrics, assessing learning styles, differentiating instruction, and creating interdisciplinary units can improve student achievement.

Our model, which blends all of these factors, is illustrated in Figure 0.1.

Figure 0.1   Blended Models

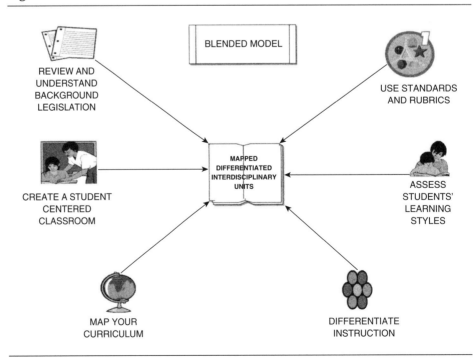

SOURCE: Diagram created in Inspiration® by Inspiration Software®, Inc.

It is important to note: This book is *not* a research tome. We present research-based practices but do not intend to delve into theory at any great length. Our interest is assisting teachers to make changes in their everyday instructional strategies by showing them how small changes made over time can have improved outcomes for students. We also have included examples that are composites of teachers' experiences and quotes from real people in the field. We hope that by reading this book you will find your own unique answer to our essential question and blend research-based practices that work for you.

Malcolm Gladwell, in his recent book *The Tipping Point* (2002), ascribes that name to a phenomenon that has three characteristics: contagiousness, the fact that little changes can have big effects, and one dramatic moment when everything changes all at once. We hope that this book can become your "tipping point" where theories and practices are linked and made easy to use.

Michelle A. Langa and Janice L. Yost

Acknowledgments

This book is the culmination of five years of teachers' self-reflection and hard work for the Rye (NH) School District. Many teachers, to whom we are extremely grateful, assisted us with our research. In particular, we would like to thank Carolyn Clithero, Kathleen Collyer, Mary Coombs, Matt Downer, Jay Forrest, Katie Jarvis, Jacqueline Reese, and Molly Rothermel, all of whom generously shared their lessons and their experiences.

We are most grateful for the trust and confidence the superintendent of Rye Schools, Dr. George Cushing, had in us as we embarked on implementing curriculum mapping, differentiated instruction, and interdisciplinary unit development.

Acknowledgement is due to Bena Kallick and Heidi Hayes Jacobs, whose research and training inspired us to implement curriculum mapping in Rye and to write this book.

We would also like to thank Patricia Underwood for her help with this book and her long-time assistance in training staff in differentiated instruction.

Finally we would like to acknowledge two editors: Faye Zucker, Corwin Press executive editor, for her enthusiasm and support during our writing process, and Courtney Langa, copy editor, whose hard work and keen eye caught all those little details that we missed.

Corwin Press acknowledges with gratitude the important contributions of the following manuscript reviewers:

William Fitzhugh
Teacher
Reisterstown Elementary School
Reisterstown, MD

Lloyd Kajikawa
Educational Consultant
Los Angeles County Office of Education
Los Angeles, CA

Douglas Llewellyn
Director of Science
St. John Fisher College
Rochester, NY

Susan Ratnoff
Special Education Coordinator
Greenland Central School
Greenland, NH

About the Authors

 **Michelle A. Langa** earned her certificate of advanced studies in educational administration from Hofstra University. Michelle has worked in the field of education since 1973. During that time, she has held positions as assistant superintendent for Pupil Services and Curriculum and Instruction, director of Special Education, executive director of two different special education nonprofit agencies, adjunct college faculty, consultant, and special education teacher. Presently, she is the curriculum coordinator for the Farmington School District in Farmington, New Hampshire.

Michelle has written several articles dealing with special education, parenting, and children's health issues for ParenthoodWeb.com and LRP-NET and is also the coauthor of another book titled *Including Families of Children With Special Needs*. Michelle has presented at state and national conferences, including the American Association of Colleges for Teacher Education.

 **Janice L. Yost** has masters' degrees in both educational administration and mathematics earned from the University of New Hampshire and Adelphi University, respectively. She is presently the principal of Rye Junior High School and has worked in the field of education for over 30 years. During that time, she has taught from sixth grade through college, and been an administrator in the middle school setting and an interim administrator in both the high school and primary school environments. She is also the president of the executive board of NH ASCD.

Jan has consulted for schools in New Hampshire and presented at local and national conferences, including the American Association of Colleges for Teacher Education.

For Fred, Courtney, and Eric, whose love and support inspired me to write and persevere, and for my parents, Vivian and Fred Cormier, who valued higher education and made me believe I could make a worthwhile contribution.

Michelle Langa

For my family and friends whose belief in me kept me going, whose patience and support allowed me to strive toward completion of this book when my will was giving out, and whose confidence in me allowed me to believe that I could do it.

Jan Yost

1

Reframing Instructional Practice for the New Challenges in Education

Maryellen's Story

Maryellen had always considered herself a master teacher. She had worked hard to get her graduate degree in elementary education after a brief stint as a high school American literature teacher. (She had gone back to graduate school once she realized that she couldn't teach literature if the students didn't know how to read. She figured if she started teaching reading to younger students, they could appreciate literature in high school.)

Maryellen thoroughly understood the requirements of the curriculum; in fact, she had chaired her school's curriculum committee for the past three years. With fourteen years of experience under her belt, she felt that she had a sound understanding of the developmental needs of students and a solid command of classroom management skills. Due to her success with students and parents, it seemed that each year her principal was giving her more challenging students, a challenge she enjoyed until this year. This year, her principal had moved her

(Continued)

(Continued)

from second grade to third grade because the principal knew that every child had to leave third grade able to read. The principal knew that Maryellen was just the teacher to accomplish this.

Maryellen's class is now 30 third graders, a few more than the recommended board policy on class size. Seven of her students are on individual education plans. Five students receive Section 504 accommodations. Six students are speakers of other languages.

Due to the diversity of student needs, Maryellen receives the assistance of a special educator on a daily basis during reading block, two Title One tutors three times a week for math, and an ESOL instructor as determined by the students' plans. The scheduling of these supplementary services had been problematic, but Maryellen worked out the kinks so as to not disrupt the flow of instruction. If nothing else, she prided herself on her resilience and determination.

At the beginning of the year, Maryellen's district introduced quarterly standardized testing to determine the students' progress. This new testing was prompted by the fact that last year her state had implemented grade-level performance standards for all students. These performance standards are the determinants of whether or not her school makes adequate yearly progress. This quarterly testing supplements the state's annual testing. In Maryellen's opinion, all this testing takes time away from instruction.

Now more than ever, Maryellen feels the weight of responsibility on her shoulders. There are so many grade-level performance standards and in every subject area: reading, writing, mathematics, science, and social studies—even the specials of music, art, and health! She doesn't even have the time to count them all. Maryellen truly doubts whether she can cover all of them, never mind have the students master them.

In addition, while she had always received one or two notes of concern from parents during each year of her teaching, the letters now are filled with complaints and there are more of them. Mostly the complaints are coming from parents of students who are average and above. These parents are angry at the intensity of services for the students in need. The parents feel that their children are being shortchanged. They keep asking Maryellen where are the enrichment activities for their students? How is she challenging these bright students? Why doesn't she have more projects involving technology and science? When is she giving these students additional time? One parent even keeps threatening to pull her child from the class and enroll him in a private school.

For the first time in her career, Maryellen feels inadequate to the demands of teaching. She realizes that things have to change. Presently, she cannot afford going back to school; after all, she has two kids of her own to support. She can buy a book. But which one should she buy? How many theories and models does she have to wade through? Where does she start?

The public is airing their opinions of the state of public education, in a *very* loud voice. Some days, the criticism of the system is so prevalent, it is hard to remember the nobility of our profession. We have heard teachers state that they do not know why they are subjecting themselves to such demeaning commentary. After all, they would like to see their critics stand up before a class of 27 sixth graders and still maintain their sanity at the end of the day! Despite how the criticism sometimes feels, we believe that it has brought about dramatic research to help us improve. Much like doctors on grand rounds, by collectively examining how and what we teach, we can produce positive results for students.

In order to understand some of the research we will present to you in this book, we believe it is important for you to understand the historical underpinnings of its development. Those underpinnings include the standards movement, the No Child Left Behind Act of 2001, and the Individuals with Disabilities Education Improvement Act of 2004.

THE IMPETUS: THE STANDARDS MOVEMENT ■

The standards movement has been gaining momentum since the 1980s, when a flurry of damaging studies regarding the state of the nation's public education system were released. The 1983 study titled *A Nation at Risk: The Imperative for Educational Reform*, prepared by the U.S. Secretary of Education and others, painted a pretty bleak view of American education. It detailed a lack of consistency among curricula, a lack of emphasis on higher order thinking skills, and a pervasive mediocrity among teachers.

The standards movement was further bolstered with the passage of the Goals 2000: Educate America Act, enacted in 1994. The act itself was the result of an Education Summit initiated by President George H. W. Bush and attended by all 50 governors. The summit underscored the nation's anxiety about the readiness of children to come to school to learn, the state of our students' performance versus other students in the world, and the lack of equitable access for *all* students to a quality education.

The act had some lofty goals, eight in all, including this one, which is most applicable to our model presented here:

(A) By the year 2000, all students will leave grades 4, 8 and 12 having demonstrated competency over challenging subject matter including English, mathematics, science, foreign languages, civics and government, economics, art, history and geography and every school in America will ensure that all students learn to use their minds well so they may be prepared for responsible citizenship, further learning and productive employment in our Nation's modern economy.

(B) The objectives for this goal are that—
(i) the academic performance of all students at the elementary and secondary level will increase significantly in every quartile and the distribution of minority students in each quartile will more closely reflect the student population as a whole

(ii) the percentage of all students who demonstrate the ability to reason, solve problems, apply knowledge and write and communicate effectively will increase substantially

(iii) all students will be involved in activities that promote and demonstrate good citizenship, good health, community service and personal responsibility

(iv) all students will have access to physical education and health education to ensure they are healthy and fit

(v) all students will be knowledgeable about the diverse cultural heritage of this Nation and about the world community (H.R. 1804, Goals 2000: Educate America Act)

Seeing this in writing concerned many a teacher and administrator. The goals seemed too overwhelming and too costly to accomplish. Not only were new curriculum and proficiency standards required, but also data collection and analysis, and preparation for, and administration of, standardized assessments.

As soon as this act was ratified, educators, administrators, school boards, and state education agencies began developing state and local curriculum frameworks that would standardize the content and assessment of what students were learning. Since the federal government reemphasized the states' control over public education with this act, we now have more than 15,000 state and local curricula governing our public schools today.

Rather than try to itemize each state's standards in this book, we believe it is important to note the findings of Strong, Silver, and Perini (2001), who analyzed the standards of 300 school districts. These researchers found that schools' standards fell into four broad categories. Those broad categories are the following:

1. **Rigor**—all students need to be able to read and understand powerful and challenging texts and the ideas that animate them.

2. **Thought**—all students need to acquire the disciplines of learning: they need to be able to collect and organize information; to speak and write effectively; to master the arts of inquiry and problem solving; and to reflect on, and learn from, their own activity as learners.

3. **Diversity**—all students need to understand their own strengths and weaknesses, their unique styles, intelligences, and cultural heritages and be able to use that knowledge to understand and work with people different from themselves.

4. **Authenticity**—all students need to be able to apply what they learn to settings beyond the school doors—especially those settings governed by the goals of citizenship and future careers.

In addition, during our own research for this book, we discovered that most of the national standards relied heavily on vocabulary contained in or similar to Bloom's taxonomy. If you examine the International Reading Association's English language arts standards, the standards of the National Council of Teachers of Mathematics or the National Science standards, they all use performance-oriented verbs such as *demonstrate*, *represent*, *problem solve*, *apply*, *evaluate*, and *analyze*. To us, this represents the major switch in emphasis from the 1980s' and 1990s' focus on self-esteem to the twenty-first-century focus on achievement.

PARADIGM SHIFT: ■
NO CHILD LEFT BEHIND ACT

January 8, 2002, will be remembered as one of the most significant days in education. On that day, President George W. Bush signed the bipartisan legislation known as No Child Left Behind. This legislation mandated new requirements for highly qualified teachers, the use of scientifically based research, stronger assessment requirements, and strict accountability rules for school districts. Those requirements forced us to reexamine the educational system as a whole. Why did this occur?

The federal government intervened for a variety of reasons:

- Studies showed that our educational system was not able to live up to all of the eight goals under the Goals 2000: Educate America Act. Most notable were the failures to improve reading scores for students in Grades 4, 8, and 12 and to improve the percentage of teachers holding a degree in their main teaching assignment.
- Extensive research gleaned from the National Assessment of Educational Progress (NAEP) indicated that, as of the 2000 administration of the test, only 28 percent of the nation's fourth graders were performing at or above proficient levels in reading and only 22 percent were performing at or above proficient levels in math.
- The Third International Mathematics and Science Study, which was administered in 1999, showed that of 38 participating countries, 18 scored higher in mathematics achievement than the United States. This caused a major embarrassment for a country that prides itself on research, development, and technology.
- Gaps in achievement between children of African American and Hispanic descent and their Caucasian peers have continued despite significant interventions such as Head Start, the nation's federally funded preschool program.
- Gaps in access to the general curriculum and achievement for English language learners and students with disabilities have remained.

Consequently, the federal government intervened with a carrot and stick approach. The carrots included flexibility in the use of federal funds, relief from teacher educational loans (up to $5,000!) for those who teach in schools serving low-income families, tax breaks for nonreimbursed purchases of classroom supplies, partnerships to improve math and science education, and funds allocated to help teachers and paraprofessionals reach highly qualified status. No one would argue that these are welcome and positive benefits for teachers.

The sticks however, were quite a surprise. The new requirements of No Child Left Behind have been translated into requirements for all teachers to be "highly qualified"; annual testing of all children in Grades 3–8 in reading and math, including new English speakers and children with disabilities; determinations of adequate yearly progress (AYP); district report cards to communities indicating if AYP has been made by their schools; and serious sanctions for those schools that have not made AYP.

Dr. George Cushing, Superintendent of Schools for four districts in New Hampshire, states,

> Top-level administrators are feeling tremendous pressure as a result of No Child Left Behind. Too many superintendents are looking to canned programs or easy fixes to improve their schools. However, that is not enough. The challenge is to bring experienced teachers around to look at the needed balance between the art and science of teaching. No Child Left Behind forces us to embrace the science of teaching by examining data. Data analysis does make a difference by showing us which students we need to target with intervention strategies. (personal communication, 2005)

Additionally, even though many teachers have years of experience, they may not meet the highly qualified status set forth in No Child Left Behind. For example, many, if not most, teachers in middle schools have elementary licensure. Depending on their teaching schedules, if they teach a particular course such as math exclusively, they are not considered highly qualified under this new law unless they hold additional licensure in mathematics. One of the hidden costs of the new law for both teachers and districts is the time and money spent to obtain "highly qualified" status.

Diane is a caring and exemplary fourth grade teacher who has been helping children learn for more than 24 years. Her home state recently issued a directive that all elementary school teachers must demonstrate competence in English, mathematics, social studies, and science by taking the PRAXIS II.

One day during her preparation period, she sadly lamented that suddenly she is not "highly qualified." She felt repudiated by the requirement. "Can you believe it? After all these years?" she said, shaking her head. The loss of her self-confidence was quite evident.

"What am I going to do? I haven't taken a standardized test since my GREs. I really am worried. I don't have the time or money to take a preparatory course for this."

We can see already that the public scrutiny of public education is intensifying as children's academic achievements are connected to high-stake consequences. As of 2004, approximately 20 states, including Alaska, California, Indiana, Massachusetts, and Oregon, mandate that if students cannot pass the state assessment test, they will be denied their high school diploma. Seventeen other states are considering the addition of similar requirements to promotion from one grade to the next.

Parents in particular have become quite concerned about their school districts' performances on these high-stakes tests. Several parents have already started class action litigation against their states and school districts, claiming that their children have been wrongly denied their high school diploma. Parents of children with disabilities are weighing in on the debate as well, as their children must take the test, albeit with accommodations. For students with learning disabilities, even under the best of circumstances, standardized testing can be daunting and quite upsetting. Ironically, these students do not often qualify for the alternate assessment and therefore must perform well on the regular tests.

SUCCESS FOR EVERY CHILD: THE INDIVIDUALS WITH DISABILITIES EDUCATION IMPROVEMENT ACT

Legislators, in reauthorizing the Individuals with Disabilities Education Act in 2004, aligned it with the No Child Left Behind Act. Denoting the emphasis on achievement, legislators renamed the act the Individuals with Disabilities Education Improvement Act.

Among the new emphases of this renewed legislation are requirements for special education teachers to be highly qualified, using up to 15 percent of entitlement funds to help struggling students *before* they are referred to special education, and requirements to consider a student's response to scientifically based programs as a factor in determining if the student has a learning disability.

In addition, children with special needs are expected to adhere to the same high standards as other children, and that means they must participate in state and local standardized tests. If a child cannot participate in a standardized test, an alternate test, with standards, must be developed to document what the child had learned.

These new requirements have necessitated a paradigm shift. Foremost, the *art* of teaching is being blended with the *science* of teaching. In our opinion, this change is a positive outcome. We must supplement our talent, educated opinions, and hard-earned experience with solid evidence of student progress, analysis of a student's skill deficiencies, and a plan to remediate and enhance skill development. While it may appear a daunting task, we can chunk the requirements into manageable pieces just as we would for our students. We can organize our strategies and design plans to achieve this. How can we do this?

In the next several chapters of this book, we can show you how to make readjustments. *We recognize that the changes we are suggesting cannot be undertaken in one semester or even a year.* We advise a carefully thought out plan to try these methods with a trusted colleague. We bet you will be surprised by the energy you will derive from learning something new. We also wager that the discovery of discussing truly important educational topics with a trusted friend will be rejuvenating. We are counting on the fact that knowing where you are heading and knowing how to get there will be a huge relief.

2

Six Factors to Help Create a Student-Centered Climate

Imagine yourself about to begin a new school year with fresh young faces, a new classroom, and a renewed energy for teaching. You're trying to figure out how you can set up your class and room to ensure learning, achievement, and respect. Many researchers have written considerable volumes about strategies for accomplishing this. We have chosen to focus on *only* six factors that are relatively easy to use. However, they do require class time and investment to implement.

Charlotte Danielson (1996), in her book titled *Enhancing Professional Practice: A Framework for Teaching*, categorized the requirements of teaching into four domains. One of these domains was called the *classroom environment*. Under this domain, Danielson described five teacher responsibilities that she considered critical to developing a community of learners. Those responsibilities are

1. creating an environment of respect and rapport,

2. establishing a culture for learning,

3. managing classroom procedures,

4. managing student behavior, and

5. organizing physical space.

We'd like to elaborate on three of these responsibilities, namely, creating an environment of respect and rapport, establishing a culture for learning, and organizing physical space. We will also add other suggestions we have learned to help you develop a student-centered climate.

■ FACTOR 1: CREATING AN ENVIRONMENT OF RESPECT AND RAPPORT

Ask people you know who was their favorite teacher and why. Invariably, you will get a response similar to "He or she cared about me." Students can sense when a teacher respects them as persons, is committed to helping them learn, and enjoys communicating with students about their love of learning and their subject area. While we all feel that this is common sense, it is reassuring to have research to validate our beliefs.

James Stronge (2002), in his book titled *Qualities of Effective Teachers*, examined a plethora of research studies and found the following:

- Teachers who create a supportive and warm classroom climate tend to be more effective with all students.
- Students associate fairness and respect with teachers being consistent and providing opportunities for students to have input into the classroom.
- Teachers' enthusiasm for learning and for the subject matter under study has been shown to be an important factor in student motivation, which is closely linked to achievement.

Other researchers have found similar factors that can make a difference in a student's desire to succeed. Dr. Russ Quaglia (2004), the Executive Director of the Global Institute for Student Aspirations, cites a "sense of belonging" as a prerequisite for a student's desire to succeed. Without it, at one extreme, students tend to drop out, or tune out. At the other extreme, at the very least, students fail to learn to the best of their potential.

Knowing that respect and rapport are critical, how can a teacher foster their development within the classroom? Here are some easy-to-implement suggestions:

1. During the first few weeks of school, take the time with your students to establish what you expect. This can be done with students from first grade to eighth grade. These short 10- to 15-minute conversations with students will pay off in the long run.

2. During these conversations, you need to demonstrate to your students that you are in charge of the classroom as the adult but that you are interested and concerned about their well-being. (Psychologists will tell you that children feel safer knowing that someone is in charge and will protect them.)

3. Help students see that learning about one another is as important as the subject matter under study. Give them time to learn about each other. Icebreaker activities such as surveys, paired conversations, treasure hunts, and so on, that identify similarities and differences in thinking

among gender, learning styles, and race are especially helpful. Not only do these activities help the students get to know one another, they are also useful in raising to the level of consciousness the stereotypes we have of individuals' learning strengths. Some of the misperceptions that can be raised are, for example, all girls excel in language arts, all Asian students excel in mathematics and music, all African Americans are good at sports, or all boys excel in science.

4. Assist students in developing norms for the classroom. This empowering behavior on your part helps students feel that their input is valued and important. In addition, students will feel ownership of the norms and therefore be more likely to adhere to them.

One of the best programs that we have used is *Responsive Classroom*, designed by the Northeast Foundation for Children (Kriete, 2002). The cornerstone of this program for developing respect and rapport within this classroom is called *morning meeting*. During this daily time period, children build community. They learn what high expectations the teacher has for them. They are given time to practice social skills and respect. Finally, teachers model care and concern for students so that they may show them to their classmates.

FACTOR 2: ESTABLISHING A CULTURE FOR LEARNING BY USING METACOGNITION

Many years ago, an advocate for a parent of a child with special needs always argued with us that our district was not meeting the needs of the student because we failed to help him develop metacognitive strategies. At the time, we were frustrated since we were using every strategy we could think of to assist this child in managing his own person, his tasks, and his materials. In retrospect, we are now grateful that the advocate turned us on to this amazing research.

Metacognition is simply described as thinking about thinking. Bena Kallick, respected author and researcher (Costa & Kallick, 2004), writes,

> Occurring in the neocortex, metacognition is our ability to know what we know and what we don't know. It is our ability to plan a strategy for producing what information is needed, to be conscious of our own steps and strategies during the act of problem solving, and to evaluate the productiveness of our own thinking.

In terms of knowing themselves as learners, even the youngest of students recognize when they feel successful at learning and when they do not. They learn pretty quickly whether they require absolute silence while studying. They learn whether they can function in a room filled with distractions. They will seek out study groups where they can discuss their understanding with a friend if it fits their style of learning. (We will delve into learning styles in detail in Chapter 5.)

Students also can figure out what learning tasks are easier for them, such as reading a fictional account of Harry Potter versus reading a paragraph on photosynthesis from a science text.

Most students learn what materials and operations they must have in place in order to accomplish a task. Pens, papers, rulers, calculators, study guides, or textbooks are all items that must be organized if a student is able to complete a required learning task. Students with attention deficit disorder constantly struggle with this piece of the learning puzzle, as they cannot manage these items very effectively.

Finally, a student must be able to decide what strategy to use to solve a learning problem. As teachers, we assume that students instinctively know how to do this or will pick it up after it is modeled by us. We can no longer assume either of those two factors is true. *Teachers need to directly instruct, model, and help students apply, generalize, and evaluate students' use of metacognitive strategies.*

How can teachers implement using metacognitive strategies in their classrooms? We believe that teachers need to thoroughly examine the strategies they use as learners themselves. Teachers should select those that are most critical to the age and subject area of the class that they are teaching. (To start off, we recommend using the same number of strategies as the grade level. For example, select four metacognitive strategies for Grade 4.)

Metacognitive Strategies

Help students think about their thinking by:

- ✓ self-questioning whether or not answers make sense;
- ✓ planning how to approach a test question or homework assignment;
- ✓ using contextual cues from texts;
- ✓ visualizing and verbalizing what they are reading;
- ✓ creating and maintaining personal dictionaries, math journals, or other ways to remember previous definitions or solutions;
- ✓ making associations between various texts, class discussions, and homework;
- ✓ chunking information into manageable sections;
- ✓ previewing new vocabulary by checking at ends of chapters and using glossaries;
- ✓ scanning material being read to look for headings, bold or italicized text, glossaries, table of contents, and so on that indicate that this information is important;
- ✓ using mnemonics devices such as Capitalization, Overall, Punctuation, and Spelling (COPS), or Survey, Question, Read, Recite, and Review (SQR3); and
- ✓ taking notes and outlining material in a way that the student determines is the best way to remember the information.

Teachers must give students knowledge of the strategy, model the strategy, and help students identify areas where the strategy should be utilized. In describing assignments to children, teachers could ask them to translate the directions in their own words and check with a peer for comprehension. Next, teachers ask students to brainstorm what strategies to use to complete the assignment. Finally, teachers and students should then evaluate the students' use of the strategy over time by incorporating the metacognitive strategy into the rubric for the assignment.

In summary, by teaching metacognitive strategies, we are enabling students by giving them lifelong problem-solving techniques for higher achievement. This is the first step in establishing a culture of achievement in the classroom. The next is using Bloom's taxonomy to assess students' knowledge.

FACTOR 3: USE BLOOM'S TAXONOMY   ■

Benjamin Bloom (1956) was a psychologist who developed a way to categorize intellectual behavior. He described six levels of thinking in a hierarchical order and asserted that most teachers only test children at the most basic level of thinking, namely the recall of knowledge. Those six levels of thinking are the following:

Figure 2.1   Bloom's Taxonomy

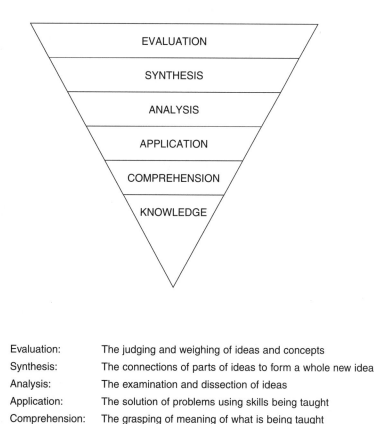

Evaluation:	The judging and weighing of ideas and concepts
Synthesis:	The connections of parts of ideas to form a whole new idea
Analysis:	The examination and dissection of ideas
Application:	The solution of problems using skills being taught
Comprehension:	The grasping of meaning of what is being taught
Knowledge:	The recall of facts, figures, and concepts

Throughout the course of this book, we will be using examples from a kindergarten life science unit that centers around seasonal changes in plants and animals, a fourth grade social studies unit involving communities and bridges, and an eighth grade algebra unit focused on variables and expressions. For the purposes of this chapter, we have developed a schematic illustrating Bloom's taxonomy using the fourth grade social studies unit as an example (see Figure 2.2).

We need to directly instruct children in achievement-oriented verbs such as those used in Bloom's taxonomy and familiarize the students with seeing and reacting to them on standardized assessments. According to Robert Marzano (2003), who studied 11 different studies on vocabulary instruction, we must not solely concentrate on memorized lists of high-frequency words. Instead, to foster higher achievement, "Students must receive direct instruction on words and phrases that are critical to their understanding of academic content" (p. 140) and "Students must be encouraged to elaborate on their understanding of new words using mental images, pictures and symbols" (p. 141). In our opinion, these findings are particularly applicable to the achievement-oriented verbs of Bloom's taxonomy since they often require understanding of nuance.

In addition, many items are missed on standardized testing because the students failed to understand the directions of the learning task. Since 40 percent of all achievement test errors are reading errors, Heidi Hayes

Figure 2.2   Illustrating Bloom's Taxonomy Using Fourth Grade Social Studies Unit

Level	Content Of Unit	Student Behaviors	Sample Verbs
Knowledge	Communities	The student will recall and define what a community is.	Recall Write Label Define
Comprehension	Communities and inventions	The student will explain the requirements for communities and inventions to succeed.	Explain Summarize Describe Illustrate
Application	Inventions	The student will design and construct a new invention, including blueprints and estimated costs.	Use Compute Apply Construct
Analysis	Communities and inventions	The student will compare and contrast the significant inventions of urban and rural communities.	Analyze Compare Contrast Separate
Synthesis	Communities	The student will create a model community with hypotheses about its industry, inventions, and needs for schools and other community services.	Create Design Hypothesize Develop
Evaluation	Communities and inventions	The students will judge each other's projects by use of rubrics and written comments.	Judge Recommend Critique Justify

Jacobs (2005), the designer of curriculum mapping, strongly believes that high-frequency words (assessment verbs such as *draw conclusions, compare and contrast*), specialized terms in context (discipline-specific vocabulary), and revising and editing skills should be part of *every* unit.

> Katie Jarvis, a middle school teacher, said, "I use Bloom's taxonomy as a tool for planning that helps me make my classroom more student centered. I want my students to go from having basic knowledge to become critical thinkers, especially in world cultures class." (personal communication, 2005)

FACTOR 4: STUDENT SELF-ASSESSMENT ■

We are keenly aware that motivating students to learn is a challenge. To assist students with motivation, teachers should give students high expectations, confidence in their ability to learn, acceptance of the place from where they are beginning as a learner, and a safe place to try new ideas. Critical to developing motivation is good assessment information that assists the students in learning from their errors. In fact, Rick Stiggins (2005), of the Assessment Training Institute, states that one of the most important aspects of assessment should be "achieving a productive, emotional response from the student." A productive emotional response, in our opinion, should give students an understanding of what they learned, what areas they still need to explore, and how to continually improve their learning behaviors.

You can design activities such as the survey in Figure 2.3 to gauge the readiness of the students to self-assess. In addition, it will lay the groundwork for the positive expectations that their parents and you have for them.

(This exercise can be used in Grades 3–8. Not only can this simple exercise lead to students' understanding of themselves but also it can serve as a starting lesson in mathematics for any grade level.)

Have the class complete the survey as homework. Each student must complete the graph himself or herself and then ask for a parent's or guardian's input. The next day, discuss the results of this survey with the class. Post their answers as a graph in the classroom. Take the time to explain to the class your expectations for them, and mark the graph. Use the graph as a motivator during the following months. Set class goals and rewards by using the rubric. Give students practice in self-assessing their work against the rubric associated with the graph. Teachers can reassess students' performances by using the same survey every three months. By doing this, students can visually see either a rise or a drop in performance.

FACTOR 5: ORGANIZING PHYSICAL SPACE ■

Noted researcher Charlotte Danielson (1996) also identifies the safety and arrangement of furniture and the use of physical resources as key factors in organizing classroom space effectively. We believe that the organization

Figure 2.3   Student Survey

Rubric for Achievement

A rubric is an explanation. In this class, four things are important to achieve your goal of becoming a good student: (1) give your best effort to learn; (2) participate in class activities; (3) respect everyone else in the classroom; and (4) complete assigned homework, and turn it in on time. The following is a rubric by which you, your parents, and _____ (*insert teacher's name here*) will determine your progress in achieving your goal.

1 = Does not give best effort to learn, does not participate in class, does not show respect for others in class, and does not turn in completed homework assignments on time.

2 = Gives some effort to learn, participates occasionally in class, has difficulty in respecting others, and struggles to turn in completed homework on time.

3 = Gives average effort to learn, participates in class on most days, is able to show respect for others on most days, and sometimes turns in completed homework on time.

4 = Gives good effort to learn, participates in class on a regular basis, is able to show respect for others every day, and turns in completed homework on most days.

5 = Gives excellent effort to learn, participates in class every day, always shows respect for others, and turns in completed homework on time.

I. On a scale of 1–5, using the rubric above, circle the number that tells me how *you* think you are as a student now.

1	2	3	4	5

II. On a scale of 1–5, using the rubric above, circle the number that tells me how your *parents* think you are as a student.

1	2	3	4	5

III. On a scale of 1–5, using the rubric above, circle the number that tells me how _____ (*insert teacher's name*) wants you to be as a student.

1	2	3	4	5

Please follow these directions:

1. Place an X next to your answers for each of the three questions.
2. Color the block containing your answer.
3. Color every block below your answer.
4. Turn and discuss these answers with your best friend.
5. Find a person in the room whom you do not know and share your answer.
6. Please save graph in your folder for future use.

	My Answer	Parents' Answer	Teacher's Answer
5			
4			
3			
2			
1			

Copyright © 2007 by Corwin Press. All rights reserved. Reprinted from *Curriculum Mapping for Differentiated Instruction, K–8,* by Michelle A. Langa and Janice L. Yost. Thousand Oaks, CA: Corwin Press, www.corwinpress.com. Reproduction authorized only for the local school site or nonprofit organization that has purchased this book.

of the classroom should reflect safe and orderly traffic patterns, comfort, and flexibility. We hypothesize that the way teachers arrange the classroom's desks and chairs reflects their comfort level in teaching and how they expect to teach (i.e., lecture, centers, group work, or flexible grouping). Think ahead about how you will organize the desks and chairs in your classroom. Does it say what you want it to?

In addition, many teachers we know are able to dazzle students with beautiful bulletin boards, exciting plays, centers, and art projects involving every imaginable object. It has been our experience that many teachers tend to become pack rats, filling their classrooms with every conceivable item that might help in learning. Unfortunately, the end result is often a cramped room that is difficult to navigate and that sends exactly the wrong message to students. We tell students to organize themselves and their materials, yet we do not always practice what we preach. Finding a means to organize what materials we need for a certain unit while storing other unnecessary materials not only demonstrates that we, as teachers, are using metacognitive strategies for organization but also removes tempting distractions for students.

Inviting and effective classroom space includes the walls as well. Each of us would be appalled to walk into a classroom that had bare walls and no student work hung up. On the other hand, it is not an infrequent occurrence to see a classroom with not an inch of wall or ceiling space bare. It is our opinion that this is just as uninviting as the bare wall.

For most students, overcrowded walls require great visual acuity and complete attention to decipher what the teacher is referring to on the wall. Thus, unless you are having a lesson on "Finding Waldo" we suggest that you use a balanced approach to wall decoration. Our first suggestion would be to hang the classroom rules for respect, behavior, and achievement; the metacognitive strategies you intend to employ; and the rubric by which assignments will be judged.

FACTOR 6: GIVE TECHNOLOGY ■ A PLACE IN YOUR CLASSROOM

Finally, give technology a permanent place in your classroom. We need to recognize that the use of computers is a daily occurrence in American life. Ian Jukes (2005), renowned speaker on technology, states,

> By the year 2010, raw information will be doubling every two weeks. How does today's prescribed curriculum prepare students to live in a world where massive amounts of information are available at the touch of a button? Learning can no longer be defined by the amount of "stuff" we know, but by how well we can access knowledge and information necessary to completing projects, inventing new approaches or solving problems. (p. 3)

Consequently, our students need exposure to and experience in using this important tool. We have some of the necessary parts already in place. Nearly every classroom in America has one or more computers. School libraries offer other media equipment, including VCRs, televisions, CD and tape players/recorders, LCD projectors, and the like. We suggest that you design your classroom space for easy access to and frequent use of technology. Make it part of the students' regular routine to be involved in either setting up or taking down pieces of equipment so that they can learn all aspects of computer usage. Incorporate the use of technology into your lesson plans and homework assignments.

In summary, to establish a student-centered classroom, focus on creating an environment of respect and rapport. Establish a culture for learning by using metacognition, Bloom's taxonomy, and student self-assessment. Design your classroom space to be inviting, free of distractions, and technology friendly. In our next chapter, we will examine the topic of curriculum mapping and why it is so important to student achievement.

Checklist for Student-Centered Classrooms

	Factors
✓	Establish high expectations at the beginning of school
✓	Inform and demonstrate to students that you are concerned for their well-being
✓	Discuss diversity and practice tolerance of others' learning styles
✓	Have students assist in developing norms for the classroom
✓	Discuss and utilize metacognitive strategies on a daily basis
✓	Use Bloom's taxonomy in direct instruction, homework assignments, and assessments
✓	Have students explain test directions to you using their own words
✓	Establish norms and practices that give students opportunities to self-assess their learning
✓	Organize physical space of the classroom to model to students the need for structure and order
✓	Decorate classroom walls with rules established with the help of students, metacognitive strategies, and rubrics for teacher and student assessments
✓	Utilize technology as an important tool for students in acquiring, managing, and analyzing information

3

Curriculum Mapping

Maryellen's Discovery

Maryellen decided that her first priority had to be developing a method for covering the state performance standards. After examining them, she realized that while the standards were close to the district's curriculum guidelines in some areas, they were not in others. (In fact, as curriculum chair for her school, she knew what that meant. The committee would have to realign the district's curriculum to meet these new expectations.)

She also realized that while the progression of the standards was linear, instruction in some areas, especially in science and social studies, didn't always flow that way. In Grades K–8, the school calendar, holidays, and even the use of certain resource materials often influenced when certain topics were introduced. After considerable thought, she decided to practice what she preached to her students: rely on your strengths. She had always been an avid diarist. Why not diary what she taught last year and just see what she had covered? Now that she was no longer responsible for second grade, she could look at it objectively without feeling anxious.

In one professional development day and on one large page of newsprint, Maryellen was able to record, using her old plan book, what units she had taught in the four core content areas and when she had taught them. She went down the hall to see an old friend and shared that newsprint with her. To her surprise, she discovered that her friend had not covered the same topics. In fact, her friend was covering some of the topics that Maryellen was teaching now.

Have you asked yourself what your students *really* studied during their previous year in school? Oh sure, you know what the curriculum guidelines say they were supposed to have learned, or maybe the items were checked off on a mastery sheet, but is that what they truly experienced? Do you know what the teacher down the hall is teaching or a teacher at the same grade level or at another school in the district? Wouldn't it be helpful to have real-time data from each of the teachers who taught the students in front of you?

When teaching for understanding, it is important to ask, "What is essential for my students to understand? What are the core concepts and skills of the unit that they should learn?" A plan to reflect on the answers to those questions is essential to guide a teacher/staff on the journey of learning and to have a clear view of students' experiences over time. Through the use of curriculum mapping, teachers now have a tool to examine the learning experiences of their students and the real educational K–12 programs within their districts. They have a vehicle for communication that allows teachers within a grade level, within a content area, across grade levels, and across content areas to look at real-time data and discuss the breadth and depth of the curriculum and the learning experiences of a child.

Curriculum maps are such communication tools, but before we get into what a curriculum map is and how it can be used, let's look at its evolution, what it is and is not. Later in the chapter we will look at how to develop a map, and the benefits for you, your students, and their parents.

■ HOW IT GOT STARTED!

In the 1970s and 1980s, curriculum leader Fenwick English developed a process for curriculum management that included mapping what content was taught, in what order, and for how long. According to English's plan, auditors collect and analyze data to ensure adherence to the curriculum and to determine the degree of alignment of the written, taught, and tested curriculum. The model has been published widely in national professional literature such as the AASA best seller *Skills for Successful School Leaders* (Hoyle, English, & Steffy, 1990).

In order to have quality control in curriculum, English's work states the importance of

> (1) a written curricular in some clear and translatable form for application by teachers in classroom or related instructional settings, (2) a taught curriculum that is shaped by and interactive with the written one, and (3) a tested curriculum that includes the tasks, concepts and skills of pupil learning which are linked to both the written and taught curricula. (Hoyle, English, & Steffy, 1990, p. 98)

Through extensive data collection in documents, interviews, and site visits and then the review of the data, the auditors are charged with determining how well a system is able to "set valid directions for pupil accomplishments and well being, concentrate its resources to accomplish those directions, and improve its performance over time" (Hoyle, English, & Steffy, 1990, p. 98).

English's pioneering work was broadened by the work of Dr. Heidi Hayes Jacobs in the 1990s. Dr. Jacobs (1997) describes curriculum mapping as "a procedure for collecting data about the actual curriculum in a school district using the school calendar as an organizer" (p. 61). The process developed by Dr. Jacobs differs from Dr. English's in that it is the individual teacher who collects the data. The teacher's data is what he or she is actually doing in the classroom in a given period of time.

CURRICULUM MAPPING   ■

In her book *Mapping the Big Picture*, Dr. Jacobs (1997) states,

> Our students need us to know their experiences over the course of time. They need us to know what's really going on in their daily classes as they move among teachers and subjects. They need us to know and give credence to their work from year to year. With that information, possibilities emerge. (p. 5)

She goes on to describe the process of collecting, analyzing, and revising the data that is compiled on a map. A curriculum map is not a lesson plan or a curriculum guideline. Rather than being the data on what a child is supposed to have experienced, it is the data on what a child *actually* experienced. Curriculum maps are living, dynamic documents that can be used, among other things, to determine the timeliness of the curriculum and the connections among disciplines.

With this collection and examination of curriculum data, teachers are better able to eliminate excessive gaps and redundancies in content; maximize conversation and communication within and between grade levels and content areas; reinforce content, skills, and assessments; align content to national, state and/or district standards; and connect assessments (products) to learning styles and strategies. Depending on availability and use of technology, curricular maps can be as complex or as simple as one wishes, but all should project the major real-time content, skills, and assessments experienced in a class and be geared to the school calendar.

WHAT HAPPENS?   ■

There are two types of maps that a teacher can develop: diary or projective. During the first phase, if teachers write a diary map, they, at a minimum, would record the content, skills, and assessments administered in their class on a daily, weekly, or monthly basis. If teachers wish to project what they will be teaching for the year, a projective map may be written for the year with editing done at regular time periods throughout the year. In either case, the teacher logs the content, or the "what" that is taught; the skills or specific processes to be mastered; and assessments or evidence used to demonstrate and measure learning. We have provided you with sample basic maps for the primary, intermediate, and junior high school levels. They are illustrated in Figures 3.1, 3.2, and 3.3.

Figure 3.1   Basic Curriculum Map, Kindergarten Science

	September	October	November
Content (noun form)	✓ Caterpillars to butterflies ✓ Early fall changes—apples	✓ Fall changes—leaves ✓ Harvest—pumpkin growth ✓ Spiders ✓ Our bones	✓ Nocturnal animals ✓ Animals prepare for winter ✓ Healthy eating, foods
Skills (verb form)	✓ Identify and sequence four stages of metamorphosis ✓ Define caterpillar, chrysalis, and butterfly ✓ Observe seasonal changes and the growth cycle of apples over the year	✓ Observe seasonal changes (leaves) ✓ Define the growth cycle of the pumpkin and other fall changes ✓ Observe spider characteristics ✓ Identify major bones in the body ✓ Define why we have bones ✓ Identify and explain healthy bone habits	✓ Discuss nocturnal vs. non-nocturnal animals ✓ Explain and identify animals that hibernate ✓ Categorize healthy foods
Assessment/ Products	✓ Drawing of a four-part sequence story about metamorphosis ✓ Dictation or recording entries into a "what I know" and "what I learned" journal ✓ Record of daily weather types on a calendar ✓ Discussion of how the weather affects the growth cycle of an apple	✓ Creation of a leaf booklet and stories ✓ Discussion of and journaling of observations during a pumpkin patch field trip ✓ Carving of jack-o'-lanterns, gathering seeds; in a journal, recording changes to a pumpkin over time ✓ Creation of spider booklets, songs, and stories	✓ Reading of literature about nocturnal animals and hibernation ✓ Acting out stories about hibernation ✓ Creation of own food pyramid using magazine pictures ✓ "Preparation" of a healthy meal on a paper plate

The second phase is a first read-through, with each teacher reading a set of school maps. Let's assume that the read-through is concentrating on content. For example, each math teacher may read the science set of maps, or Grade 4 teachers read the maps for Grades 3 and 5 with the purpose of looking for potential areas of revision and gaining new information, or the language arts teachers read the Grade 8 mathematics maps to check for literacy requirements.

Next, a diverse group of about a half-dozen faculty members reads the maps of the entire school. The question is, what are they looking for? At this small-group review, teachers are looking to gain knowledge and share the findings from the second phase. It is at this point that educators can identify when and if a specific concept is being taught in all classes at a grade level or being taught in some classes at several grade levels.

Have you ever thought, why do some of my students recognize how to change a decimal to a percentage and others are absolutely lost? Or perhaps some of your students have experience in a specific research technique such as IIM, while others have no idea what you are talking about.

Figure 3.2   Basic Curriculum Map, Grade 4 Social Studies

	January	February	March
Content (noun form)	✓ Connections—bridges	✓ Community	✓ Inventions
Skills (verb form)	✓ Apply basic geometry skills ✓ Use geometric terms correctly (right angle, acute angle, obtuse angle, line segment) ✓ Identify and describe four bridges from literature ✓ Research information on types of bridges ✓ Compare and contrast various types of bridges, such as suspension and drawbridge	✓ Describe types of communities ✓ Locate on a map or globe the continents, and the states and major cities of the U.S. ✓ Describe the physical landscape of the regions of the U.S. ✓ Compare and contrast communities in the U.S. ✓ Identify the positive and negative aspects of living in a community ✓ Prepare and present an oral report	✓ Describe how past inventions affect our lives ✓ Predict some possible inventions of the future ✓ Develop a new invention or improve on an existing invention ✓ Measure for accuracy ✓ Apply computational skills (addition, subtraction, multiplication [up to two-digit multiplier], and division [one-digit divisor])
Assessment/ Products	✓ Diary of mathematical steps in bridge construction ✓ Recording and defining associated vocabulary ✓ Completion of the writing prompt, "This bridge leads to the future . . ." ✓ Construction of a model bridge	✓ Teacher observation ✓ Weekly quizzes and reviews ✓ Teacher-prepared test ✓ Individual project ✓ Portfolio ✓ Exhibits	✓ Teacher observation ✓ Weekly quizzes and reviews ✓ Teacher-prepared test ✓ Individual project ✓ Portfolio ✓ Exhibits

Or maybe you are about to start a unit on metamorphosis and butterflies and the students say, "We've done that!" Have they? Through a small-group review of the curriculum maps, your questions can be answered.

During this small review phase, another area that may be examined is the type of assessments being used. Do the assessments address different learning styles? Are they all paper-and-pencil tests? The goals throughout the third phase are to identify areas of concern, to compile the data, and to share the findings.

In the fourth phase, or large-group review, the entire faculty comes together to hear the findings of the small groups. The faculty examines the results and identifies patterns. Once the faculty has examined and analyzed the data, it is time to identify those areas that can be revised immediately with relative ease and those that need more study, research, and time.

Given that a curriculum map is a continuous work in progress, the updating of maps and review process should be continuous; thus the cycle begins again.

We hope the chart in Figure 3.4 gives you a visual interpretation of the curriculum mapping process.

Figure 3.3   Basic Curriculum Map, Grade 8 Algebra

	September	October	November
Content (noun form)	Preview of algebra	Rules of algebra	Rational and irrational numbers
Skills (verb form)	✓ Evaluate algebraic expressions ✓ Find the prime factorization of a number ✓ Follow the order of operations when evaluating an expression ✓ Use sets of numbers to solve equations and inequalities ✓ Organize information in solution sets, ordered pairs, and matrices ✓ Draw the graph of an equation by making a table of values and using ordered pairs ✓ Translate words into algebraic symbols and vice versa	✓ Recognize equalities, expressions, and inequalities ✓ Simplify expressions ✓ Find solutions to equations ✓ Recognize equivalent equations ✓ Use inverse operations to solve equations ✓ Use the properties of equality ✓ Use substitution ✓ Use the distributive property ✓ Solve application problems ✓ Use properties of equality, operations, and identities	✓ Classify numbers ✓ Compute with signed numbers ✓ Use inequality symbols with real numbers ✓ Graph inequalities ✓ Add like terms with signed coefficients ✓ Multiply matrices
Assessment/ Products	✓ Homework ✓ Class participation ✓ Quizzes ✓ Graphing activities ✓ Probability activities ✓ Math journal ✓ Tests	✓ Homework ✓ Class participation ✓ Quizzes ✓ Math journal ✓ Tests	✓ Homework ✓ Class participation ✓ Quizzes ✓ Math journal ✓ Tests

NOT THE ENTIRE SCHOOL OR DISTRICT! HOW ABOUT A TEAM?

Of course, there is always the possibility that your school district or school is not ready to implement curriculum mapping, so how can you as an individual or team use this valuable tool? Grade-level teams, content-area teams, or interdisciplinary teams can use curriculum maps as a communication tool, as a basis for curricular planning and discussion, and as a tool to improve the quality of instruction. At the end of this chapter is a checklist for a procedure of how this can be accomplished.

■ WHY WRITE A CURRICULUM MAP?

Parents who are moving into the community often ask us what is taught in our schools. We can easily send them a copy of our curriculum maps so they can see when and what specific content is covered, what skills are expected to be mastered, and how the curriculum is aligned to the state frameworks.

Figure 3.4 Cycle of Curriculum Mapping

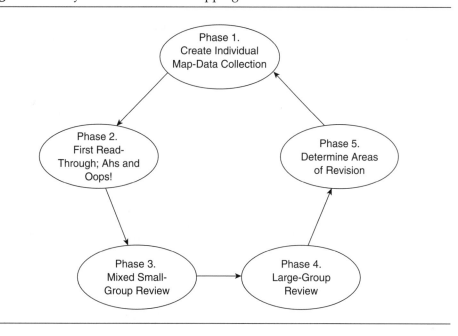

But the use of a curriculum map goes beyond the ability to inform potential new community members. As a teacher in a system or school that maps their curricula, you can look at the maps of the teachers of grade levels that come before the one in which you teach and gain insight into the students' experiences. You can also look at the maps of teachers of grade levels that follow to see what your students' learning experiences will be and, perhaps, adjust your curriculum accordingly.

A curriculum map provides insight into the continuum of your students' individual experiences. A team of teachers can build on interdisciplinary connections, and parents can enhance their child's learning experience by talking to their child about a book the child is reading in your class or take the child to a location you are studying in geography because the parents have been informed through the curriculum map. The maps can be used by teachers at a common grade level to determine whether or not students at that grade level are having similar educational/content and skills experiences during the year.

Curriculum maps are communication tools that can be given to teachers new to a specific grade level or content area, to parents for informational purposes, to teachers and administrators at sending or receiving schools, and to a faculty for long-range planning, to allow districts to determine if all areas of the standards are taught. Curriculum maps are communication, planning, and teaching tools.

WHAT ABOUT STATE AND NATIONAL STANDARDS? ■

The standards and curriculum alignment can be an overwhelming and frustrating task to complete and ensure, but by taking it a bit at a time and

Figure 3.5   Checklist of Steps for Curriculum Mapping

_____1.   Determine the set of standards and benchmarks to which the curriculum will be aligned.

_____2.   Determine what content area will be mapped. (We recommend that the primary or elementary team concentrate on one content area such as mathematics or social studies.)

_____3.   As a team, agree on the format for mapping (Figures 3.1 through 3.3 are examples of calendar-based maps) and whether diary or projective maps will be completed.

_____4.   Individually, team teachers should complete the content, skills, and assessment sections of their map. Each teacher should label/align each content or skill entry with a standard or benchmark. (There should be no discussion during this phase of the process since the purpose is to get a picture of what the curriculum looks like as it is currently taught.)

_____5.   Begin the review process by having each teacher review all maps for redundancies, gaps, and ahas.

_____6.   Conduct a discussion on findings. (At this point, there can be discussions about student achievement data, areas of strength and weakness, alignment to standards and/or benchmarks, a common vision for teaching and learning, and places for integration).

_____7.   Edit maps and practices based on discussion.

_____8.   Continue the process.

Copyright © 2007 by Corwin Press. All rights reserved. Reprinted from _Curriculum Mapping for Differentiated Instruction, K–8,_ by Michelle A. Langa and Janice L. Yost. Thousand Oaks, CA: Corwin Press, www.corwinpress.com. Reproduction authorized only for the local school site or nonprofit organization that has purchased this book.

using your maps, it can be manageable. The first step is identifying what set of standards will be used.

Are they state-mandated frameworks or standards, content-specific national standards, or district benchmarks? Once that has been determined, it is time to review the skills written on a curriculum map and label each concept or skill with the standard or benchmark that it meets. It will be evident whether or not there is misalignment with the standards and whether or not the standards are being met. We will cover this topic in greater detail in our next chapter.

In summary, curriculum mapping provides the reality-based data needed to carry on conversations about curriculum and the challenges associated with it. It does not tell a teacher how to teach, but is a tool used to look at what is being taught and how it is being assessed. Since curriculum mapping is always a work in progress, schools that are continuously reviewing are making adjustments to meet the needs of their students and looking critically at teaching and learning.

4

Using Standards
and Rubrics

The new demand for accountability requires that teachers understand and utilize state standards. Since the implementation of No Child Left Behind, many states require that students master their state's standards in order to graduate. Since the onset of this high-stakes testing, questions have arisen as to how teachers judge students' achievement toward those state standards. No longer is it acceptable to grade a student's work with an A or a D; teachers must now be able to demonstrate that they have a consistent and defensible assessment paradigm.

In this chapter, we will show you ways to incorporate state standards with your curriculum maps. This inclusion not only will assist teachers and parents in understanding the chosen material but also will assist students in understanding what is expected of them. We will also provide an explanation of rubrics and samples of assessment rubrics that can be used across several content areas.

USING STANDARDS TO DEVELOP ■
CURRICULUM MAPS, UNITS, OR THEMES

Most states have established curriculum standards and performance standards, or what are commonly referred to as benchmarks, for each of the major academic areas. States frequently have incorporated standards developed by organizations such as the National Council of Teachers of English, which wrote the English Language Arts Standards; the National Council of the Teachers of Mathematics, which produced the National Mathematics Standards and Expectations; the National Research Council, which created the National Science Education Standards; and the National Council for the Social Studies, which developed the Curriculum Standards for Social Studies.

Curriculum standards are simply statements of what is to be taught. Performance standards, or benchmarks, are articulated expectations for what students must demonstrate after exposure to the required content.

In our opinion, teachers must use state standards to plan lessons and as the basis for assessment. Mark O'Shea (2005), researcher and professor of education, promotes the benefits of using state standards in lesson planning. He argues,

- State standards clarify local priorities for student learning.
- State standards help ensure that, for the first time, high-stakes tests actually measure the curriculum that is being taught.
- The achievement gap between underperforming students and their more privileged counterparts is closing in many states where standards are well developed.
- National and state accountability movements are based on student achievement of state standards.
- National textbook publishers have begun to align their products with state standards.

To us, using a standard is akin to graphing a series of concentric circles to plan.

By examining Figure 4.1, you can see that using standards is at the center of planning a map, unit, or theme. In their book *Understanding by Design,* Wiggins and McTighe (1998) suggest that if teachers want a certain outcome, they must identify it first and then design backward the instructional experiences to reach that outcome.

For example, using the content listed in our Basic Kindergarten Science Map (see Figure 3.1), you can see that in September through November, the children will be studying organisms' change over time using the topics of insect metamorphosis and the growth cycle of a fruit. Parents might

Figure 4.1   Using Standards to Plan a Unit or Theme

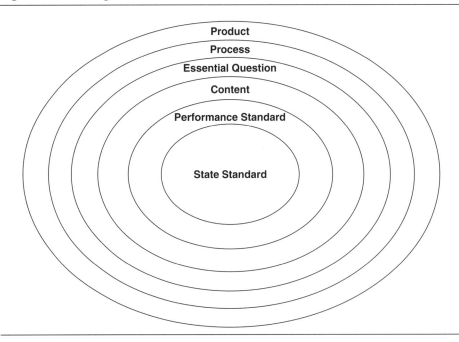

wonder why the teacher chose these particular topics. If the teacher developing that map had inserted a state standard for science (New Hampshire State Curriculum Frameworks for Science, Plymouth State University, 1995, currently under revision), which reads, "Students will demonstrate an increasing ability to understand how environmental factors affect all living systems (i.e., individuals, community, biome, and biosphere) as well as species to species interactions," parents may be able to figure out the connection. However, if the teacher also inserted the local performance standard, which reads, "By the end of grade two, students will be able to: Name plants and animals whose appearance changes in different seasons and describe the differences" (SAU 50 Science Curriculum, 2004), parents could easily recognize why these topics were chosen and why these lessons are important.

The new curriculum map would look like this:

Figure 4.2   Intermediate Curriculum Map, Kindergarten Science

	September	October	November
State/Local Standard	Students will demonstrate an increasing ability to understand how environmental factors affect all living systems (i.e., individuals, community, biome, and biosphere) as well as species-to-species interactions.	Students will demonstrate an increasing ability to understand how environmental factors affect all living systems (i.e., individuals, community, biome, and biosphere) as well as species-to-species interactions.	Students will demonstrate an increasing ability to understand how environmental factors affect all living systems (i.e., individuals, community, biome, and biosphere) as well as species-to-species interactions.
State/Local Performance Standard	By the end of Grade 2, students will be able to name plants and animals whose appearance changes in different seasons and describe the differences.	By the end of Grade 2, students will discuss features that help plants and animals survive in different environments or in the same environment during different seasons.	By the end of Grade 2, students will be able to observe and describe objects and make comparisons.
Content	✓ Caterpillars to butterflies ✓ Early fall changes—apples	✓ Fall changes—leaves ✓ Harvest—pumpkin growth ✓ Spiders	✓ Nocturnal animals ✓ Animals prepare for winter
Skills	✓ Identify and sequence four stages of metamorphosis. ✓ Define caterpillar, chrysalis, and butterfly. ✓ Observe seasonal changes and the growth cycle of apples.	✓ Observe seasonal changes (leaves). ✓ Define the growth cycle of the pumpkin and other fall changes. ✓ Observe spider characteristics.	✓ Discuss nocturnal vs. non-nocturnal animals. ✓ Identify at least three animals that hibernate. ✓ Describe the habitats of hibernating animals.
Assessment/ Products	✓ Drawing of a four-part sequence story about metamorphosis ✓ Dictation or recording of entries into a "what I know" and "what I learned" journal ✓ Record of daily weather types on a calendar ✓ Discussion of how the weather affects the growth cycle of an apple	✓ Creation of a leaf booklet and stories ✓ Discussion of and journal of observations during a pumpkin patch field trip ✓ Carving of jack-o'-lantern, gather seeds; in a journal, record of changes to a pumpkin over time ✓ Creation of spider booklets, songs, and stories	✓ Retelling of the stories "The Legend of Sleeping Bear" by Wargin and "Bears Make Rock Soup" by Erdrich ✓ Drawing of a story about sleeping bears and present it to class ✓ Acting out stories about hibernation ✓ Creation of a song about sleepy animals

We realize that achieving this standard will require a plethora of lessons over many themes or units since there are numerous instructional concepts involved.

Using our other basic maps, if we include the state and local performance standards (New Hampshire Department of Education, 1993a, 1993b), they would look like this:

Figure 4.3   Intermediate Curriculum Map, Grade 4 Social Studies

	January	**February**	**March**
State/Local Standard	Students will demonstrate an understanding of the connections between systems, the consequences of the interactions between human and physical systems, and changes in distribution and importance of resources.	Students will demonstrate an understanding of the meaning, rights, and responsibilities of citizenship as well as the ability to apply their knowledge of the ideals, principles, organization, and operation of American government through the political process and citizen involvement.	Students will demonstrate the ability to analyze the potential costs and benefits of economic choices in market economies, including wants and needs; scarcity; tradeoffs; and the role of supply and demand, incentives, and prices.
State/Local Performance Standard	By the end of Grade 6, students will identify and discuss ways people depend on, use, and alter the physical environment.	By the end of Grade 6, students will discuss why it is important to participate in community and government affairs.	By the end of Grade 6, students will explain that individuals and households undertake a variety of activities, including producing, consuming, saving, and investing, in order to satisfy their economic needs and wants.
Content	✓ Bridges	✓ Community	✓ Inventions
Skills	✓ Apply basic geometry skills. ✓ Use geometric terms correctly (right angle, acute angle, obtuse angle, line segment). ✓ Identify and describe four bridges from literature. ✓ Research information on types of bridges. ✓ Compare and contrast various types of bridges, such as suspension and drawbridge.	✓ Define what constitutes a community. ✓ Describe types of communities. ✓ Describe how the physical landscape is a contributing factor in the development of communities. ✓ Describe the physical landscape of the regions of the U.S. ✓ Locate on a map five major cities of the U.S. that were influenced by the physical landscape.	✓ Describe how past inventions affected our lives. ✓ Predict some possible inventions of the future. ✓ Develop a new invention or improve on an existing invention. ✓ Measure for accuracy. ✓ Demonstrate understanding of Newton's laws of motion.
Assessment/ Products	✓ Pretest of existing knowledge ✓ Diary of mathematical steps in bridge construction ✓ Record of and definitions of associated vocabulary ✓ Writing prompt completed: "This bridge leads to the future..." ✓ Two-page report on a particular type of bridge ✓ Proper use of geometric terms ✓ Completed geometry packet ✓ Teacher-prepared test ✓ Model bridge ✓ Observations made by teacher	✓ Pretest of existing knowledge ✓ Oral report ✓ Weekly quizzes ✓ Teacher-prepared test ✓ Exhibit illustrating four types of communities ✓ Observations made by teacher	✓ Pretest of existing knowledge ✓ Construction or illustration of new invention or improvement to an invention ✓ Oral report or videotape describing the improvement of an existing invention or the development of a new invention ✓ Teacher-prepared test ✓ Observations made by teacher

Figure 4.4   Intermediate Curriculum Map, Grade 8 Algebra

	September	October	November
State Standard	By the end of Grade 12, students will use algebraic concepts and processes to represent situations that involve variable quantities with expressions, equations, inequalities, matrices, and graphs.	By the end of Grade 12, students will use algebraic concepts and processes to represent situations that involve variable quantities with expressions, equations, inequalities, matrices, and graphs.	By the end of Grade 12, students will develop number sense and an understanding of our numerations system.
Performance Standard	✓ Simplify algebraic expressions using the standard order of operation. ✓ Evaluate algebraic expressions for given values of the variable and formal algebraic methods. ✓ Use tables and graphs as tools to interpret expressions, equations, and inequalities. ✓ Perform simple operations on matrices.	✓ Simplify expressions involving grouping symbols and containing rational numbers and integer exponents. ✓ Solve equations and inequalities in one or two variables, by informal and formal algebraic methods. ✓ Demonstrate a conceptual understanding of equality. ✓ Apply properties and field operations to solve problems and simplify computation and demonstrate conceptual understanding of field properties.	✓ Demonstrate an understanding of the relative magnitude of numbers. ✓ Compare and order real numbers. ✓ Read and write rational numbers. ✓ Graph the solution set of equations and inequalities in one variable.
Content	Preview of algebra	Rules of algebra	Rational and irrational numbers
Skills	✓ Evaluate algebraic expressions. ✓ Follow the order of operations when evaluating an expression. ✓ Use sets of numbers to solve equations and inequalities. ✓ Organize information in solution sets, ordered pairs, and matrices. ✓ Draw the graph of an equation by making a table of values and using ordered pairs. ✓ Translate words into algebraic symbols and vice versa.	✓ Recognize equalities, expressions, and inequalities. ✓ Simplify expressions. ✓ Find solutions to equations. ✓ Recognize equivalent equations. ✓ Use inverse operations to solve equations. ✓ Use the properties of equality. ✓ Use substitution. ✓ Use the distributive property. ✓ Solve application problems. ✓ Use properties of equality, operations, and identities.	✓ Classify numbers. ✓ Compute with signed numbers. ✓ Use inequality symbols with real numbers. ✓ Graph inequalities. ✓ Add like terms with signed coefficients. ✓ Multiply matrices.
Assessment/ Products	✓ Homework ✓ Class participation ✓ Quizzes ✓ Graphing activities ✓ Math journal ✓ Tests	✓ Homework ✓ Class participation ✓ Quizzes ✓ Math journal ✓ Tests	✓ Homework ✓ Class participation ✓ Quizzes ✓ Math journal ✓ Tests

You will notice that the maps for older students contain different standards for each month, as the students are able to proceed at a faster pace than the younger ones.

Teachers might wonder how they will cover the entire compendium of standards. It may seem like an impossible task. However, we want to assure you that it is not. We examined ten states: California, Florida, Kentucky, Massachusetts, Michigan, Minnesota, New Hampshire, North Carolina, Oregon, and Texas. In the majority of states that we studied, state education departments have moved toward individual grade level proficiency standards or expectations, beginning with the content areas of language arts and mathematics. They are working on the other content areas, but for now these standards are grouped by primary (K–2 or K–4), intermediate (5–6 or 5–8), and secondary benchmarks (9–10 or 9–12).

Obviously, for our purposes, grade-level expectations are the easiest for teachers to use. Teachers can simply list the state or local curriculum and performance standards on their curriculum map, determine the content as to how to teach that standard, and then proceed to design the skills and assessments. Teachers can then share that map with other teachers for feedback.

The task becomes a little more complicated if you live in a state that uses larger groupings of proficiency standards, such as Grades K–4, Grades 5–6, and so on, or primary, intermediate, and secondary. All the grade teachers contained in a particular grouping (i.e., K–4) must discuss what standards will be covered in what grade level. While the task may seem daunting at first, the ensuing conversations from such a discussion are actually quite reinvigorating for teachers.

These discussions lead to reduction of redundancies in the curriculum, the shoring up of gaps, and the improvement of instruction overall. Progress we all want to see! Imagine the thrill of knowing that you are presenting material to students that has not been covered in other classes! It is the sure way to end the annoying "We already learned that" statements from students.

> Patricia Underwood, an educational consultant, when discussing the use of standards, states, "I have noticed two important changes: (1) There is much more accountability in grade level teams, and (2) there is a more logical progression of curriculum standards through the grades." (personal communication, 2005)

But how do you assess progress toward those proficiency standards? The answer lies in the development of rubrics.

RUBRICS

Every experienced teacher has a mind-set or framework as to what constitutes an excellent, good, fair, or poor grade. However, communicating that mind-set to students and parents is often difficult. Parents and students have long complained of teachers' lack of consistency in grading from product to product, from classroom to classroom, and from one grade to the next. Teachers have also struggled in tying assessments to improved instruction and helping students become more adept at self-assessment.

Recently, one teacher from Louisville, Kentucky (Kenney, 2005), was suspended due to the lack of consistency in her grading procedures. Students in her class lost points for improperly labeling assignments and failing to properly file papers in correct folders. If this teacher had established at the beginning of her class the performance criteria by which she intended to judge her students, she would not have found herself in the position of being suspended. She needed to inform her students that organization of their material was an important aspect of their grade. What would have helped her? The plain and simple answer is having rubrics.

According to Arter and McTighe (2001), rubrics are "scoring tools containing criteria and a performance scale that allows us to define and describe the most important components that comprise complex performances and products" (p. 8).

With multiple choice, true/false, or matching questions and answers, teachers, students, and parents recognize that there is only one correct response. The difficulty lies with constructed response assessments such as essays, speeches, plays, and projects. Teachers need to explicitly state what is being judged and what will constitute each of the grades being assigned. This is not an easy task!

Because we know you have limited time, we recommend that teachers develop what is known as a *general rubric,* one that can be used across similar performances regardless of the content. It is also the easiest rubric to use. Arter and McTighe (2001) have developed simple steps and recommendations in developing a rubric. First and foremost, it is important to keep in mind a metarubric for rubrics: content, clarity, practicality, and technical soundness. They suggest a three-point scale with 3 = ready to roll, 2 = on its way but needs revision, and 1 = not ready for prime time.

They suggest that teachers gather samples of student work; sort the work into piles by judging the product as strong, average, and weak; and then write down what were the indicators in the student's work that made the teacher sort it into one of the three piles. Next, teachers should look for common attributes among each pile and label them as traits. Examples of traits include understanding the content, analysis of topic, problem solving, organization of material, and delivery of presentation. (If the student work is primarily a writing piece, rubrics contained in the Six Traits for Writing or the John Collins Writing Program are both very helpful.)

It is important to compare the traits gained from this activity to those listed in the state standards. One would hope that they are similar. The next step in the process is to write a *value-neutral statement* of what the trait is. Teachers can help reinforce what they mean by providing samples to students of what is a strong, average, or weak example of the trait being discussed. Repeated direct instruction in what constitutes each level of the trait being discussed will be necessary.

Using our curriculum map for eighth grade math in Chapter 3, we developed a rubric for judging math journals.

1. First, we sorted students' work into four piles; we chose to use the terms of advanced, proficient, basic, and novice (our state's rubric on our annual state assessment).

2. We developed a set of traits that we thought important to the unit being studied.

3. We tackled the value-neutral statements. We have to admit that we struggled with these. However, we believe that we achieved a set with which we could work.

4. We wrote an explanation of the traits and gave specific examples to directly instruct students.

Our rubric and the description of the traits are listed next.

Using Figure 4.5, we can see that teachers would have to directly instruct students as to what is meant by "Understanding/Application of Concept" and the levels of performance on the scale. In addition, in writing a rubric, it is imperative to give solid examples and to use language appropriate to the reading level of the students who will be using it. By using appropriate reading levels, teachers will be encouraging students to use the rubric as a self-assessment of their own work, prior to handing the project in for teacher grading. In terms of our example above, we chose language suitable to the reading level of an eighth grade student. In checking the readability level of our rubric, we found that on the Flesch-Kincade grade level score, an eighth grade student in the ninth month of school should be able to read it without too much difficulty. (The Flesch-Kincade grade level score is a mechanism to judge the readability of written work. It is contained in Microsoft Word and can be accessed by clicking on the Tools menu and then Spelling/Grammar.)

Rubrics not only help with consistency and communication, they also serve as an important guide for students. Jay McTighe (1997) said, "When students have opportunities to examine their work in light of known criteria and performance standards, they begin to shift their orientation from 'What did I get?' to 'Now I know what I need to do to improve'" (p. 6). Hopefully, that is the goal of every teacher, to create and nurture the desire to improve in each student.

As for those in the primary grades, teachers would be wise to use two rubrics: one for parents and one for the children. Single, simple sentences, combined with a drawing or stickers, would enable young students to understand what is expected of them, while setting the stage for use of rubrics throughout their academic careers. Using more appropriate language, including the definition of your state's criteria for acceptable performance, would help parents see what lies ahead. Examples of primary rubrics for both parents and children for the kindergarten science map we developed are shown in Figures 4.6 and 4.7.

Jacquie Reese, a sixth grade language arts teacher, summed up the case for rubrics. She said, "In the last five years, I would not think of giving a project without a rubric. It is the best way for students to determine their own grades. It gives them ownership. If they truly follow the steps of the rubric, they can get an A" (personal communication, 2005).

Figure 4.5   Rubric for Math Journal

Trait	4 Advanced	3 Proficient	2 Basic	1 Novice
Understanding/ Application of Concept	✓ You demonstrated that you know the concept. ✓ You are able to apply the concept to multiple problems.	✓ You demonstrated that you know the concept most of the time. ✓ You are able to apply the concept to at least three problems.	✓ You demonstrated you still have a hard time identifying the concept. ✓ You are only able to apply the concept to the problem at hand.	✓ You were unable to demonstrate that you know the concept. ✓ You were unable to apply the concept.
Use of Operations/ Calculations	✓ You identified all elements of the problem. ✓ You selected the proper operation at least 95% of the time. ✓ You correctly calculated the problem at least 95% of the time.	✓ You identified some but not all elements of the problem. ✓ You selected the proper operation at least 80% of time. ✓ You correctly calculated the problem at least 80% of the time.	✓ You identified one of the elements but not all the elements of the problem. ✓ You selected the proper operation at least 65% of the time. ✓ You correctly calculated the problem at least 65% of the time.	✓ You were unable to correctly identify any elements of a problem. ✓ You selected the proper operation less than 65% of the time. ✓ You correctly calculated the problem less than 65% of the time.
Evidence of Problem-Solving Strategies and Explanation of Solution	✓ You wrote at least five sentences explaining your choice of operation and logic for strategy. ✓ You provided correct representations at least 95% of the time.	✓ You wrote at least three sentences explaining your choice of operation and logic for strategy. ✓ You provided correct representations at least 80% of the time.	✓ You wrote one sentence explaining your choice of operation and logic for strategy. ✓ You provided correct representations at least 65% of the time.	✓ You were unable to write any sentence explaining your choice of operation and logic for strategy. ✓ You provided correct representation less than 65% of the time.

Understanding/Application of Concept: In math, a concept is an idea or method to help categorize or calculate numbers. Understanding the concept means that you are able to correctly explain it in your own words. Applying the concept means that you are able to choose and use the correct idea in math.

Example: The distributive property of mathematics is a concept. It involves numbers that are added and then multiplied by another number. (It does not involve subtraction or division.) You distribute (spread out) the multiplier over the numbers to be added. If you were given an example of $n = 4(6 + 4)$, you must be able to correctly explain the concept at work. You must know that the distributive property is required in this example. Applying the concept means that you correctly choose and use the concept in equations. In this example, using the distributive property would look like this: $n = 4 \times 10$. Another way to calculate the answer using the distributive property is $n = 4 \times 6 + 4 \times 4$. Either way, the correct answer is 40.

In the rubric, you will be judged on how well you understand (are able to explain) and apply (choose and use) the concept (idea).

(Continued)

Figure 4.5 (Continued)

Use of Operations/Calculations: An operation changes numbers in six ways: addition, subtraction, multiplication, division, raising to powers, and taking roots. In order to choose an operation, you must first figure out the elements of the problem. What is the problem asking you to do? Second, it is important to change numbers in the right way by choosing the correct operation. To calculate means to determine an answer.

Example: Steve has 12 video games that he purchased for $49.00 per game. What is his total profit if he sells the 12 games for $52.50 each? What is his total profit if he decides to sell 3 of the games to his friends at cost?

In this example, you must first figure out what the problem is asking you to do. It is asking you to figure profit, which means sale price minus cost. You must choose the correct operation (way to change numbers) to determine what Steve paid for the games. You would multiply 12 × $49.00 for a total cost of $588.00. You would also need to multiply 12 games by $52.50 for a total sale of $630.00. To figure his total profit, you would need to determine (calculate) to subtract his cost of $580.00 from his sales of $630.00 for a correct answer of $42.00.

In the second part of the example, if Steve chose to sell 3 of the games to his friends at cost, you would need to choose the correct operation of multiplication of the 3 games by Steve's cost of $49.00. You would also need to multiply 9 games by his new sales price of $52.50. You would then add both of these answers together for a correct answer of $619.50. His profit would be figured then by subtracting his cost of $588.00 from the total of his sales, $619.50. The answer is $31.50.

This problem required you to choose seven separate operations to determine the two answers.

In the rubric, you will be judged on choosing the correct operation (the way you change the numbers) and calculate (determine) the correct answer.

Evidence of Problem-Solving Strategies and Explanation of Solution: Part of every mathematical problem involves trying different ways to solve the problem. Often, there are many ways to solve a problem. To show evidence of problem-solving strategies (operations you used to solve a problem) is as important as the correct answer. It is also equally important that you explain your solution (tell how you reached the answer that you did).

Example: In the first part of the above problem, you could have chosen other operations to correctly determine the answer. If you had determined the profit on each game first, by subtracting the old price of $49.00 from the new price of $52.50, you would have reached an answer of $3.50 per game. You could have then multiplied the individual profit of $3.50 per game times the 12 games, for a correct answer of $42.00. Either way to solve the problem is correct. By writing out your solution, you are showing that you know how to solve the problem and are showing how you reached your answer.

In the rubric, you will be judged on your evidence of problem-solving strategies (showing how to solve the problem) as well as your explanation of your solution (how you reached the answer that you did).

Figure 4.6 Parent Rubric for Kindergarten Science

Trait	Advanced	Proficient	Basic	Novice
	A student at this level demonstrates a thorough understanding of information, concepts, and skills. The student uses scientific knowledge to solve problems. The student uses a variety of tools (i.e., drawings, text, and graphs) to communicate scientific data.	A student at this level demonstrates an overall understanding of information, concepts, and skills. The student is familiar with procedures used in science. The student uses scientific knowledge to examine problems. The student clearly communicates scientific data.	A student at this level demonstrates reasonable understanding of information concepts and skills. The student is familiar with the procedures used in science.	A student at this level demonstrates some understanding of information concepts and skills. The student is aware that scientific information is gained from observations and experiments.
Ask Questions (Inquires about the concept being studied)				
Know the Answer (Has grasped the concept of life science under study)				
Use Technology to Observe Nature (Is able to use instruments to observe and measure)				
Record What You Saw or Found (Is able to draw, dictate, or otherwise represent his or her knowledge)				

SOURCE: Created by RJH teachers: K. Collyer, M. Coombs, M. Downer, J. Forrest, and J. Reese. Reprinted with permission from the Rye (NH) School Board.

Figure 4.7   Student Rubric for Kindergarten Life Science

Trait	Advanced	Proficient	Basic	Novice
Ask Questions				
Know the Answer				
Use What You Know				
Use Technology to Observe Nature				
Record What You Saw or Found				

SOURCE: Created by RJH teachers: K. Collyer, M. Coombs, M. Downer, J. Forrest, and J. Reese. Reprinted with permission from the Rye (NH) School Board.

For a rather extensive listing of Web sites to help you develop your rubrics, please refer to http://school.discovery.com/schrockguide/assess.html or http://www.rubrician.com/general.htm

In summary, using standards and rubrics are guaranteed methods to ensure that your teaching is aligned to the state frameworks and is defensible for assessment purposes. They also can be used to communicate to students and parents the requirements of the curriculum and the school's focus on student achievement.

In our next chapter, we will demonstrate how to assess students' learning styles and needs.

5

Assessing Students' Learning Styles and Needs

Maryellen Starts Examining the Puzzle

The 30 third graders facing Maryellen are a puzzle. With so many of them requiring accommodations, she can't give individual attention in the way that she would like. Maryellen had always experimented with flexible grouping, mostly as an afterthought in science and social studies. She had always grouped children in reading and math; but unless there was dramatic progress, the children usually stayed in their groups throughout most of the year.

However, she now realized that flexibly grouping children, according to their needs and the way they learn, would have to be her priority. She began to investigate what would be the best approach. With so many models to choose from, where should she start?

So often in a school's mission and belief statements we see a phrase such as "all students can learn." Yet, in planned lessons, there appears to be more emphasis put on a delivery that is for the auditory or visual learner, or for children who learn through the verbal/linguistic or logical/mathematical intelligences. With few exceptions, we focus on a narrow range of learning styles or intelligences. Since we need to address the needs of all our students, or truly live by the words "all students can learn," as educators we must recognize that it is just as important to know *how* a child learns as it is to know what he or she learns.

■ GARDNER'S MULTIPLE INTELLIGENCES

In 1983, Howard Gardner of Harvard University introduced his theory of multiple intelligences in his book *Frames of Mind.* In it, he suggests that intelligence is not merely a single, discrete number (IQ) that is determined by the answers to a series of items on a test and measures primarily an individual's verbal and mathematical abilities. Rather, he proposes that humans possess many intelligences and that the mind's problem-solving capacities are multifaceted. In his work, Gardner promotes that human intelligence includes verbal-linguistic, logical-mathematical, visual-spatial, bodily-kinesthetic, musical, interpersonal, and intrapersonal components, each developing at different times and at different degrees in each human.

In 1999, Dr. Gardner added the naturalist intelligence to his original list of seven intelligences.

As educators, Gardner's theory of multiple intelligences makes sense when we think about our students and their talents. Why is it that one student can solve a complex mathematical problem, yet cannot draw a still-life composition? Why is it that one student works well in a group setting, yet another prefers to work alone? Why is it that when students are asked to assemble a project, one will read the directions first, another will review the diagrams first, while a third will look at the pieces and try to figure out how the pieces fit? Trish Underwood, a New Hampshire consultant, states, "Of all the learning style models out there, Gardner's Multiple Intelligence model gives me concrete things to do with kids. When a kid is misbehaving, I switch to another intelligence and usually get better results" (personal communication, 2005).

■ MULTIPLE INTELLIGENCES AND BLOOM'S TAXONOMY

In his book *Multiple Intelligences in the Classroom,* Thomas Armstrong (2000) proposes and gives several examples of where multiple intelligence

Figure 5.1   Multiple Intelligences

Verbal-Linguistic	Logical-Mathematical	Visual-Spatial	Bodily-Kinesthetic
Has the ability to use words and language. Learns through reading, writing, and speaking.	Has the ability to use reason, logic, and numbers. Learns through making pattern connections and computation.	Has the ability to perceive visually. Learns through pictures and image manipulation.	Has the ability to control body movement. Learns through use of both gross and fine motor skills.
Musical	**Interpersonal**	**Intrapersonal**	**Naturalist**
Has the ability to produce and appreciate music. Learns through sounds and rhythms.	Has the ability to relate to others. Learns through working collaboratively.	Has the ability to self-reflect. Learns through working alone.	Has the ability to categorize things and observe nature. Learns though collecting and studying a group of objects.

activities incorporate all of Bloom's taxonomy levels. He provides several grids that show a teacher how to identify specific tasks in a lesson to the multiple intelligences (linguistic, logical-mathematical, spatial, bodily-kinesthetic, musical, interpersonal, and intrapersonal) and to Bloom's taxonomy levels (knowledge, comprehension, application, analysis, synthesis, and evaluation).

While Gardner's theory categorized different intelligences, and Armstrong's blending of multiple intelligences with Bloom's taxonomy was insightful, neither approach helped teachers understand *how* children learn.

SILVER, HANSON, AND PERINI'S ■
FOUR CATEGORIES OF LEARNING STYLES

Many researchers delved into this interesting puzzle. Among them were Harvey Silver, Robert Hanson, and Matthew Perini (2000). They developed a useful method of classifying learners according to their preference for a particular way of thinking.

The individual components of Silver, Hanson, and Perini's categories are sensing, intuitive, thinking, and feeling.

1. Sensing people are those who gather facts through the use of their senses: seeing, hearing, smelling, touching, and tasting. They verify their facts and make judgments based on those facts. They tend to solve problems through established processes.

2. Intuitive people are those who gather information through discovery and relationships. They like innovation and dislike repetition.

3. Thinking people are those who think in terms of cause and effect, logical and verifiable information.

4. Feeling people are those who base judgments on how they feel, on likes and dislikes, and on stimuli other than logic.

Silver, Hanson, and Perini developed four basic categories of learning styles. They are the following:

1. Sensing-Thinking Learners (ST)—organized, efficient, active learners who focus more on ideas than people. They must be kept busy and be given immediate feedback. These learners typically prefer step-by-step instructions, a clear understanding of what is expected of them, and the opportunity to apply learned skills and activities or assessments in which there is a right or wrong answer as opposed to open-ended or interpretative.

2. Intuitive-Thinking Learners (NT)—logical probers who want to understand complex problems. Facile with language, they are able to speak, debate, and write extensively on a subject they have studied. These learners are always asking why and looking for logical relationships.

3. Intuitive-Feeling Learners (NF)—highly imaginative, unconventional students who prefer to follow their own path to learning. Tending to be nonconformists, this group dislikes rules and routines. They are learners who need self-expression and excel when allowed to use original ideas and solutions when problem solving.

4. Sensing-Feeling Learners (SF)—emotionally involved students who are interested in learning about situations concerning living things rather than cold, hard facts. Ever helpful, they care deeply about people and need to interact with others while learning by sharing ideas. These students excel in a cooperative learning environment.

How can these learning styles be applied to a classroom setting? Whether you are developing activities, developing assessment tools, or planning a lesson, elements that will address the learning styles of the students can be incorporated.

1. Sensing-thinking learners typically prefer direct instruction and demonstrations. Activities should be developed that are based on recitation, facts, and organization and that answer the questions who, what, or where.

2. Intuitive-thinking learners prefer activities that require them to be analytical and evaluative and that answer the question, why. They enjoy comparing and contrasting, summarizing, or hypothesizing about concepts and ideas.

3. Intuitive-feeling learners prefer tasks in which they may be creative, artistic, and inventive. They want to be involved and be allowed to relate the concepts to their own life.

4. Sensing-feeling learners want to be involved in activities in which cooperation and verbal interaction are emphasized. They want to have the opportunity to find out how others feel about the concept and share ideas.

■ DETERMINING INTELLIGENCES AND LEARNING STYLES

There are several learning style inventories, such as the Dunn and Dunn learning style model of instruction, Gregoric's mediation abilities model, the 4-MAT system, and Myers-Briggs personality traits, that can be used to assist you in determining a child's most highly developed intelligence or learning style. But to get a more comprehensive understanding of a child, an inventory is only one factor. Observations, school documentation, and discussions with other teachers, a child's parents, and the student should also be part of determining a child's learning profile. These are all important facets in assessing how a child learns and maximizing the learning process. So how can this be accomplished? Armstrong (2000) details ways in which to get information about students. Here are a few examples from which you can select.

1. Learn about yourself. What is your learning style and predominant intelligence(s)?

2. Learn about the child from the previous year's teachers. Did the child prefer to use models or diagrams (the visual-spatial intelligence)? Did the child do best when learning through lectures (the auditory learner)? Is the child successful in PE class and/or does the child engage in at least one sport on a regular basis (bodily-kinesthetic intelligence)? Can the child easily compute numbers or search for patterns and logical sequences (logical-mathematical intelligence)? Does the child prefer working in groups (interpersonal intelligence) or alone (intrapersonal intelligence)?

3. Talk with parents about their child and their child's interests beyond the school day.

4. Depending on their age, have students complete an inventory (see Figure 8.5) and through some medium (written, verbal, picture, or physical interpretation) learn about their interests and/or how they think they learn best.

5. Review school documentation. In what subjects did a child excel? In what subjects did a child have difficulty either academically and/or behaviorally?

Completing some or all of the above suggestions will give you a picture of who is before you in a class. A final thought is to keep a log or journal of observations and discussion outcomes. We do understand that the greater the number of students you teach in a day, the more difficult it is to accomplish this suggestion.

INTEGRATING MULTIPLE INTELLIGENCES, BLOOM'S TAXONOMY, AND LEARNING STYLES INTO THE CURRICULUM

Figure 5.2 is a grid we developed for a sixth grade unit on *Pirate: Fact vs. Fiction*, in which an array or menu of assessments are listed. For each intersection of an intelligence on the horizontal axis with a category in Bloom's taxonomy on the vertical axis, we could assign a dominant learning style to the cell. The learning styles are denoted by the abbreviations ST, meaning sensing-thinking learner; SF, meaning sensing-feeling learner; NT, meaning intuitive-thinking learner; and NF, meaning intuitive–feeling learner.

For example, in the cell that is the intersection of the multiple intelligence *logical/mathematical* with Bloom's taxonomy category of *analysis*, we have placed the instructional product *analyze a typical pirate's diet and identify deficiencies in vitamins and minerals*. Given that we are asking the student to analyze a dilemma to determine the deficiencies in each diet, the student who may select to complete this product would most likely have an intuitive-thinking (understanding) learning style as dominant.

Once we completed the grid, we wanted to ensure that all learning styles were represented both horizontally and vertically. As a classroom teacher, it would be time-consuming to generate such an extensive matrix, but developing a partial grid in which you address multiple intelligences, learning styles, and Bloom's taxonomy is feasible.

Figure 5.2 Instructional Products Using Multiple Intelligences, Bloom's Taxonomy, and Learning Styles

	Verbal-Linguistic	Logical-Mathematical	Visual-Spatial	Musical-Rhythmic	Bodily-Kinesthetic	Naturalist	Interpersonal	Intrapersonal
Evaluation	Create a poem explaining the hazards of a pirate's life. **NF**	Rate three different nautical logs for accuracy of ships' positions. **ST**	Critique one of the pirate films seen in class. **NT**	Rate your favorite sea shanty and describe why. **ST**	Pretend you are a judge. How would you try to judge *The Black Pirate?* **NF**	Explain the effect of global warming on the Isles of Shoals. **ST**	Prepare a defense for a pirate in front of your peers. **SF**	Explain how your opinion has changed or stayed the same in regard to pirates. **NF**
Synthesis	Examine how piracy supported various governments; write an article on findings. **ST**	Given a beginning location and destination, winds, and supplies, project the length of a voyage. **NT**	Design a large mural using information learned about pirates. **NF**	Burn a CD containing sea shanties and sea songs. **SF**	Design and assemble a mobile depicting pirate life. **NF**	Organize a list of plant or wildlife that existed in the 17th century and is now extinct. **ST**	Summarize the relationship between a pirate ship captain and his crew. **NT**	Plan a field trip that would demonstrate what you learned in this unit. **NT**
Analysis	Compare the stories of Celia Thaxter as presented by S. Voss with a story telling of B. Macintosh. **NT**	Analyze a typical pirate's diet and your own diet. Identify the deficiencies in vitamins and minerals of each diet. **SF**	Compare the traits of the main characters of the movies *The Black Pirate* and *Lethal Weapon.* **NT**	Classify shanties by historical period. **ST**	Create a clay model of a pirate; explain the different aspects/uses of what pirates wore. **NF**	Categorize at least five sea animals by genus and species. **ST**	Debate the stereotype of a pirate's life vs. the facts. **NF**	Share your opinion of pirate life before and after this unit. **SF**

	Verbal-Linguistic	Logical-Mathematical	Visual-Spatial	Musical-Rhythmic	Bodily-Kinesthetic	Naturalist	Interpersonal	Intrapersonal
Application	Write and illustrate a pirate ABC book. **ST**	Develop a set of plans for a pirate ship model. **NF**	Design pirate clothing for a mannequin. **SF**	With two or three friends, perform a musical skit about how those on board a ship being attacked felt. **SF/NF**	Construct a pirate ship model. **NT**	Investigate ecological issues on the Isles of Shoals. **NT**	Survey the class to design a board game on piracy. **ST**	Write a letter to a loved one as a captive on a pirate ship. **SF**
Comprehension	Write a letter to a classmate to describe what the horse latitudes, trade winds, and doldrums are. **SF**	Create a game in which the players must convert U.S. currency into Spanish doubloons. **NF**	Sequence pictures of pirates and piracy into a story. **ST**	Demonstrate on drums various rhythms used by the men in the galley while rowing. **NT**	Identify flags of nations that existed in the 17th century. **ST**	Classify at least 10 plants found on the Isles of Shoals and create a photo journal. **NF**	Report on the perception of your classmates regarding piracy. **SF**	Share your feelings regarding the Isles of Shoals experience. **SF**
Knowledge	Make a chart of pirate facts learned. **ST**	Make a list of diseases sailors were subject to while at sea. **ST**	Create a chart with pictures of pirates and when they lived. **NT**	Recite three sea shanties to help others understand life at sea. **SF**	Label the sections of a galleon model. **ST**	Identify five oceans/seas frequented by pirates. **ST**	Quote three pirates and survey peers for reaction to the quotes. **NT**	Recall the interesting facts that you learned from speakers. **ST**

From the grid, we then developed task cards from which the students could select the type of task they most enjoyed and the ones that led to a successful and challenging learning experience.

In the final chapter of this book, we will provide examples of the detailed task cards used in the unit (see Figures 8.8–8.25).

6

Differentiated Instruction

MAJOR TEACHER PLANNING MODELS ■

Three major instructional models have dominated the last 50 years in education. Researchers have written tomes about *mastery learning*, as proposed by John Carroll and Benjamin Bloom in 1971; *mastery teaching*, as developed by Madeline Hunter in 1982 (and updated in 2004); and *a framework for teaching*, developed by Charlotte Danielson in 1996. We are sure that each of these three models has fans, as each model has been revised and updated recently. While all three models were developed years ago, in our humble opinion they are just as useful today, especially in this era of accountability.

MASTERY LEARNING

John Carroll and Benjamin Bloom (yes, the same gent who developed the famous taxonomy) felt that giving students time to master new material before moving on to the next set of learning objectives was more of a critical factor than any other factor in teaching. Carroll defined aptitude as the length of time it takes a person to attain mastery of a subject. He believed that all children could learn, given the time and proper instruction to do so. Mastery learning as defined by these two researchers involves teachers:

- respecting and teaching to individual learner characteristics,
- having specific objectives,
- dividing the lesson into small chunks in a sequential fashion,

- using a multitude of teaching and assessment strategies to ensure mastery,
- preceding each unit with a pretest, and
- concluding with a posttest to provide information for future lessons.

J. Ronald Gentile and James Lalley (2003) have developed a revised version of mastery learning. Essentially, Gentile and Lalley recommend the following:

1. Each lesson is located in the context of a spiraling curriculum, so that lessons build on prior knowledge while establishing a base for new concepts.

2. Prerequisite skills are clearly identified so that an anticipatory set can be designed to activate students' memories.

3. Lessons must be taught in a variety of ways.

4. Rubrics containing the objectives for mastery are clearly written and given to students.

5. Teachers use a wide variety of assessments to ascertain students' mastery.

6. Teachers and the school administration develop a plan to remediate those students who fail to reach mastery.

This model presents sound theoretical constructs for teachers and is noteworthy for its use of scaffolding and rubrics and concentration on remediation if initial teaching fails.

MASTERY TEACHING

Madeline Hunter (2004) provided another way to view instruction. In 1982, she developed a format for making teaching decisions. In a nutshell, the most salient features of the format for teachers are

- knowing the content and instructional objective for the lesson;
- knowing what the performance standard is and the underlying learning prerequisite skills;
- providing a hook, called an *anticipatory set,* to motivate students;
- presenting the material—teacher input, modeling the material for students;
- teaching students to remember, transfer, and use the information independently;
- checking for understanding;
- providing guided practice to students in the new material;
- using Bloom's taxonomy to extend students' thinking;
- closing the lesson by reviewing the salient concepts presented; and
- providing independent practice through individual or group classwork, homework, or projects that require the student to apply the materials to new situations.

Her seminal work influenced thousands of teachers throughout the last two decades and is still viable today.

DIFFERENTIATED INSTRUCTION

A Framework for Teaching

Finally, Charlotte Danielson (1996) developed her framework for teaching by identifying 22 components of professional practice, which she divided into four domains: planning and preparation, classroom environment, instruction, and professional responsibilities. For our purposes here, we will focus on Domain 1: planning and preparation.

Each component of the domains is accompanied by several elements and a rubric to indicate a teacher's level of performance. The framework also contains an excellent self-assessment to assist teachers in examining their own work in relationship to the framework.

For the domain of planning and preparation, there are six components with 20 elements. They are the following:

1. Demonstrating knowledge of content and pedagogy
   - Knowledge of content
   - Knowledge of prerequisite relationships
   - Knowledge of content-related pedagogy

2. Demonstrating knowledge of students
   - Knowledge of characteristics of age group
   - Knowledge of students' varied approaches to learning
   - Knowledge of students' skills and knowledge
   - Knowledge of students' interests and cultural heritage

3. Selecting instructional goals
   - Value
   - Clarity
   - Suitability for diverse students
   - Balance

4. Demonstrating knowledge of resources
   - Resources for teaching
   - Resources for students

5. Designing coherent instruction
   - Learning activities
   - Instructional materials and resources
   - Instructional groups
   - Lesson and unit structure

6. Assessing student learning
   - Congruence with instructional goals
   - Criteria and standards
   - Use for planning

Danielson's work has been adopted by many districts throughout the country because of its specificity and ease of use. It has also become the basis for a new paradigm in teacher evaluation.

We value elements of each of the models presented here. However, as practitioners, we have found that using the most salient features of each model and blending them into a cohesive whole is most beneficial to teachers and their students. Figure 6.1 compares each of these models with the features that we are proposing in our blended model.

Figure 6.1   Comparison of Major Lesson Planning Models: Mastery Learning, Mastery Teaching, a Framework for Teaching, and Our Blended Model

Key Factors	Mastery Learning	Mastery Teaching	Framework for Teaching	Blended Model
Teacher Preparation	Demonstrate and practice respect for individual learner characteristics	Consciously identify teaching decisions in content, student behavior, and teaching behavior	Demonstrate knowledge of content and pedagogy	**Self-reflect on practice** **Obtain "highly qualified status" of NCLB**
Knowledge of Students	Activate students' prior memories	Provide a hook called an anticipatory set to motivate students	Demonstrate knowledge of students	**Use information gleaned from creating a student-centered climate and investigating learning styles and multiple intelligences**
Design of Lessons	Identify prerequisite skills	Know the objective for the lesson	Select instructional goals	**Develop essential questions** **Map your curriculum for content, skills, and assessment**
Standards	Write rubrics containing objectives for mastery	Know what the performance standard is	Communicate standards to students	**Use your local curriculum or state frameworks** **Create and use rubrics**
Instruction	Build on prior knowledge Present lessons in a variety of ways	Presenting the material: provide teacher input, modeling for students, checking for understanding Provide guided practice to students in new material	Design coherent instruction	**Use Bloom's taxonomy** **Differentiate content and process** **Create interdisciplinary units**
Assessment	Use a wide variety of assessments, including pre- and posttesting of material	Provide independent practice through individual/group classwork, homework, or projects	Assess student learning	**Create and use rubrics** **Differentiate products, including homework** **Give students time for self-assessment**
Reteaching	Spiral curriculum to reinforce applicability of prior knowledge to new concept Develop plan for remediation	Close the lesson by reviewing the salient concepts presented	Emphasize problem-based learning	**Group students flexibly based on need** **Provide additional practice through differentiated homework**

Whichever method you choose to design your instruction, it is critical to have a method in mind. Those who rely on experience, instinct, or "winging it" will find it very hard to succeed in today's teaching environment.

Once teachers have planned their instruction, established a student-centered environment, mapped the curriculum, established the practice of using rubrics, and learned about their students' learning styles, it is time to investigate ways of reaching *all* students in the classroom.

RESEARCH-BASED INSTRUCTIONAL PRACTICES ■

For years, Dr. Robert Marzano of the Mid-Continent Research for Education and Learning Institute (MCREL) has advocated the use of research-based instructional strategies. He, Debra Pickering, and Jane Pollock (2001) conducted a meta-analysis of studies and found that the existing research supported nine instructional strategies as having positive effects on student learning. Those nine strategies follow:

1. Identifying similarities and differences

2. Summarizing and note taking

3. Reinforcing effort and providing recognition

4. Homework and practice

5. Nonlinguistic representations

6. Cooperative learning

7. Setting objectives and providing feedback

8. Generating and testing hypotheses

9. Providing questions, cues, and advance organizers

In our opinion, one of the key factors to higher student achievement is providing questions that not only check for factual accuracy but also promote deeper understanding and continuing inquiry. How does one frame such questions? One way is to examine Wiggins and McTighe's definition of essential questions.

ESSENTIAL QUESTIONS ■

Wiggins and McTighe (1998), building upon the work of the Essential Schools Coalition, defined essential questions as "provocative and multilayered questions that reveal the richness and complexities of a subject" (p. 28). Their research suggests that essential questions can be described as having three purposes: to expose the core of a subject, to serve as a repeating unifier to a unit thus leading to a more in-depth understanding, and to lead to further inquiries. Essential questions represent the big ideas of a unit and do not have an obviously right answer. The intent of the question is to sustain student interest throughout the unit. Significantly, essential questions are always on the analysis, synthesis, and evaluation steps of Bloom's taxonomy.

To illustrate how essential questions can be easily woven into your lessons, we have developed essential questions to accompany the three maps we have been illustrating throughout this book. By adding essential questions and a listing of resources and technology that you may need for a lesson, you have created what we have termed a *complex map*. Here are our examples:

Figure 6.2   Complex Curriculum Map, Kindergarten Science

	September	**October**	**November**
State/Local Standard	Students will demonstrate an increasing ability to understand how environmental factors affect all living systems (i.e., individuals, community, biome, and biosphere) as well as species-to-species interactions.	Students will demonstrate an increasing ability to understand how environmental factors affect all living systems (i.e., individuals, community, biome, and biosphere) as well as species-to-species interactions.	Students will demonstrate an increasing ability to understand how environmental factors affect all living systems (i.e., individuals, community, biome, and biosphere) as well as species-to-species interactions.
State/Local Performance Standard	By the end of Grade 2, students will be able to name plants and animals whose appearance changes in different seasons and describe the differences.	By the end of Grade 2, students will discuss features that help plants and animals survive in different environments or in the same environment during different seasons.	By the end of Grade 2, students will be able to observe and describe objects and make comparisons.
Essential Questions	Do all things change with the seasons?	Can pumpkins grow in Alaska?	How do animals know when it is time to sleep?
Content	✓ Caterpillars to butterflies ✓ Early fall changes—apples	✓ Fall changes—leaves ✓ Harvest—pumpkin growth ✓ Spiders	✓ Nocturnal animals ✓ Animals prepare for winter
Skills	✓ Identify and sequence four stages of metamorphosis. ✓ Define caterpillar, chrysalis, and butterfly. ✓ Observe seasonal changes and the growth cycle of apples.	✓ Observe seasonal changes (leaves). ✓ Define the growth cycle of the pumpkin and other fall changes. ✓ Observe spider characteristics.	✓ Discuss nocturnal vs. non-nocturnal animals. ✓ Identify at least three animals that hibernate. ✓ Describe the habitats of hibernating animals.
Assessment/ Products	✓ Drawing of a four-part sequence story about metamorphosis ✓ Dictation or record of entries into a "what I know" and "what I learned" journal ✓ Record of daily weather types on a calendar ✓ Discussion of how the weather affects the growth cycle of an apple	✓ Creation of leaf booklet and stories ✓ Discussion and journal of observations during a pumpkin patch field trip ✓ Carving of jack-o'-lantern, gather seeds; a journal record of changes to a pumpkin over time ✓ Creation of spider booklets, songs, and stories	✓ Retelling of the stories class has read aloud ✓ Drawing of a story about sleeping bears presented to the class ✓ Acting out stories about hibernation ✓ Creation of a song about sleepy animals
Technology	✓ Video: *On the Wings of the Monarch* (2001)	✓ http://lessonplancentral. com/lessons/Science/ Animals/Insects/index.htm	✓ http://www.national geographic.com/kids
Resources	✓ Calendars ✓ Science journals ✓ Books: *Summer* by R. Hirschi; *Nature All Year Long* by C. Walker Leslie	✓ Calendars ✓ Science journals ✓ Pumpkins ✓ Books: *Year at Maple Hill Farm* by A. Provensen and M. Provensen; *Red Leaf, Yellow Leaf* by L. Ehlert	✓ Calendars ✓ Science journals ✓ Books: *The Legend of Sleeping Bear* by K. Wargin; *Bears Make Rock Soup* by L. Erdrich; *Berlioz the Bear* by J. Brett

Figure 6.3   Complex Curriculum Map, Grade 4 Social Studies

	January	February	March
State/Local Standard	Students will demonstrate an understanding of the connections between systems, the consequences of the interactions between human and physical systems, and changes in distribution and importance of resources.	Students will demonstrate an understanding of the meaning, rights, and responsibilities of citizenship as well as the ability to apply their knowledge of the ideals, principles, organization, and operation of American government through the political process and citizen involvement.	Students will demonstrate the ability to analyze the potential costs and benefits of economic choices in market economies, including wants and needs; scarcity; tradeoffs; and the role of supply and demand, incentives, and prices.
State/Local Performance Standard	By the end of Grade 6, students will identify and discuss ways people depend on, use, and alter the physical environment.	By the end of Grade 6, students will discuss why it is important to participate in community and government affairs.	By the end of Grade 6, students will explain that individuals and households undertake a variety of activities, including producing, consuming, saving, and investing, in order to satisfy their economic needs and wants.
Essential Questions	Why do we build bridges? Are bridges necessary?	Do we need communities?	What makes a good invention?
Content	Bridges	Community	Inventions
Skills	✓ Apply basic geometry skills. ✓ Use geometric terms correctly (right angle, acute angle, obtuse angle, line segment). ✓ Identify and describe four bridges from literature. ✓ Research information on types of bridges. ✓ Compare and contrast various types of bridges, such as suspension and drawbridge.	✓ Define what constitutes a community. ✓ Describe types of communities. ✓ Describe how the physical landscape is a contributing factor in the development of communities. ✓ Describe the physical landscape of the regions of the U.S. ✓ Locate on a map five major cities of the U.S. that were influenced by the physical landscape.	✓ Describe how past inventions affected our lives. ✓ Predict some possible inventions of the future. ✓ Develop a new invention or improve on an existing invention. ✓ Measure for accuracy. ✓ Demonstrate an understanding of Newton's laws of motion.
Assessment/ Products	✓ Pretest of existing knowledge ✓ Diary of mathematical steps in bridge construction ✓ Record and definition of associated vocabulary ✓ Completion of the writing prompt, "This bridge leads to the future…" ✓ Proper use of geometric terms ✓ Completion of geometry packet	✓ Pretest of existing knowledge ✓ Preparation and presentation of an oral report ✓ Weekly quizzes ✓ Teacher-prepared test ✓ Production of an exhibit illustrating four types of communities ✓ Observations made by the teacher	✓ Pretest of existing knowledge ✓ Construction of or illustration of the new invention or the improvement to an invention ✓ Preparation and presentation of an oral report or videotape describing the improvement of an existing invention or the development of a new invention
Technology	✓ Physics Balsa Bridge Building Contest online: http://www.balsabridge.com/ ✓ *Building Big: Bridges*, by D. Macauley, WGBH Boston, VHS or DVD	✓ Kids and Communities: http://www.planning.org/kidsandcommunity/	✓ Video: *Golden Jubilee 24 Karat Collection Road Runner/Wile E. Coyote: The Classic Chase* (1990) by Warner Brothers
Resources	✓ Balsa bridge-making kits ✓ Books: *Bridge to Terabithia*, by K. Paterson (1987); *Bridges: From My Side to Yours*, by J. Adkins (2002)	✓ United States map ✓ Books: *What is a Community from A to Z?* by B. Kalman (1999); *City Green* by D. DiSalvo-Ryan (1993); *Map Mania: Discovering Where You Are & Getting to Where You Aren't* by M. Di Spezio and D. Garbot (2003)	✓ Books: *Imaginative Inventions: The Who, What, Where, When, and Why of Roller Skates, Potato Chips, Marbles, and Pie (and More!)* by C. Harper (2001); *Time For Kids: Benjamin Franklin, A Man of Many Talents* by Editors of *TIME For Kids* (2005)

Figure 6.4   Complex Curriculum Map, Grade 8 Algebra

	September	October	November
State Standard	By the end of Grade 12, students will use algebraic concepts and processes to represent situations that involve variable quantities with expressions, equations, inequalities, matrices, and graphs.	By the end of Grade 12, students will use algebraic concepts and processes to represent situations that involve variable quantities with expressions, equations, inequalities, matrices, and graphs.	By the end of Grade 12, students will develop number sense and an understanding of our numerations system.
Performance Standard	✓ Simplify algebraic expressions using the standard order of operation. ✓ Evaluate algebraic expressions for given values of the variable and formal algebraic methods. ✓ Use tables and graphs as tools to interpret expressions, equations, and inequalities. ✓ Perform simple operations on matrices.	✓ Simplify expressions involving grouping symbols and containing rational numbers, and integer exponents. ✓ Solve equations and inequalities in one or two variables, by informal and formal algebraic methods. ✓ Demonstrate a conceptual understanding of equality. ✓ Apply properties and field operations to solve problems and simplify computation and demonstrate conceptual understanding of field properties.	✓ Demonstrate an understanding of the relative magnitude of numbers. ✓ Compare and order real numbers. ✓ Read and write rational numbers. ✓ Graph the solution set of equations and inequalities in one variable.
Essential Questions	How are algebraic concepts and processes used to represent everyday situations?	How are algebraic concepts and processes used to represent everyday situations?	How big/small is a number?
Content	Preview of algebra	Rules of algebra	Rational and irrational numbers
Skills	✓ Evaluate algebraic expressions. ✓ Follow the order of operations when evaluating an expression. ✓ Use sets of numbers to solve equations and inequalities. ✓ Organize information in solution sets, ordered pairs, and matrices. ✓ Draw the graph of an equation by making a table of values and using ordered pairs. ✓ Translate words into algebraic symbols and vice versa.	✓ Recognize equalities, expressions, and inequalities. ✓ Simplify expressions. ✓ Find solutions to equations. ✓ Recognize equivalent equations. ✓ Use inverse operations to solve equations. ✓ Use the properties of equality. ✓ Use substitution. ✓ Use the distributive property. ✓ Solve application problems. ✓ Use properties of equality, operations, and identities.	✓ Classify numbers. ✓ Compute with signed numbers. ✓ Use inequality symbols with real numbers. ✓ Graph inequalities. ✓ Add like terms with signed coefficients. ✓ Multiply matrices.
Assessment/ Product	✓ Homework ✓ Class participation ✓ Quizzes ✓ Graphing activities ✓ Math journal	✓ Homework ✓ Class participation ✓ Quizzes ✓ Math journal ✓ Tests	✓ Homework ✓ Class participation ✓ Quizzes ✓ Math journal ✓ Tests
Technology	✓ Excel spreadsheet to collect data		✓ "How the West Was Negative One" by Sunburst
Resources	✓ Class openers	✓ Class openers	✓ Class openers

In our opinion, the major planning models described earlier, the research-based effective instructional strategies, and essential questions fit neatly with Tomlinson's model of differentiated instruction.

DIFFERENTIATED INSTRUCTION ■

Carol Ann Tomlinson (2001), in her book *How to Differentiate Instruction in Mixed Ability Classrooms*, states, "Differentiated Instruction is so powerful because it focuses on concepts and principles instead of predominantly on facts. Teachers who differentiate instruction offer minimal drill and practice of facts (as these practices tend to create little meaning or power for future learning); they focus instead on essential and meaningful understanding to create transferable learning power" (p. 74). Differentiation allows students to learn at different levels using a variety of activities (some whole class, some small group, and/or some individual) that meet their learning styles. It maximizes student learning by determining a student's entry level and helping him or her progress through a variety of experiences based on his or her needs. It should be noted that this is not an individual educational plan, but rather approaches or activities that meet the needs of students with similar learning styles and entry levels.

There are three areas in which a teacher may differentiate: content, process, and/or product. Tomlinson (1999) defined *content* as what the teacher wants the students to learn and the materials or mechanisms through which that is accomplished, *process* as the activities designed to ensure that students use key skills to make sense out of essential ideas and information, and *products* as vehicles through which students demonstrate and extend what they have learned. (Since many researchers use different terms in their work, we would like our readers to think of the term *content* used by both Tomlinson and Hayes Jacobs as the subject matter or unit being taught. Tomlinson describes *process* as the methods in which students acquire skills, whereas Hayes Jacobs is more interested in describing what those units of ability truly are. Tomlinson's *product* is akin to Jacobs' *assessment*.)

Tomlinson further defines *readiness* as a student's entry point relative to a particular understanding or skill; *interest* as a child's affinity, curiosity, or passion for a particular topic or skill; and *learning profile* as how a child learns.

When differentiating instruction, there are times when whole-group activities are appropriate, and there are times when small-group or individual activities are appropriate. The teacher is the guide, offering students tasks and activities that are appropriate for their readiness, interests, and learning styles.

The following is a schematic for differentiating instruction:

Figure 6.5   Differentiation Process

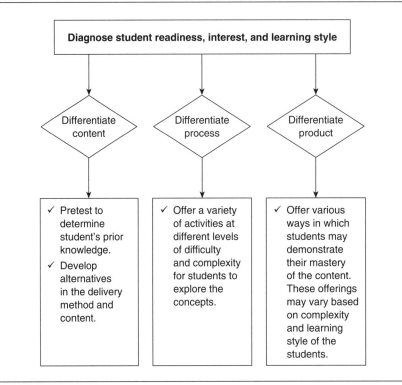

Content

When differentiating content, there are a variety of possibilities, some of which are

- selecting a variety of books and resource materials from which students may select or be assigned based on their reading ability,
- selecting specific areas of interest within the focus of a unit (*interest groups*),
- compacting the curriculum for advanced learners in the focus area,
- developing learning contracts with your students,
- developing groups of learners based on their readiness or interest,
- reteaching to small groups of students who need additional support or further explanation and exempting those students who have already mastered the topic,
- establishing learning centers or stations, and
- allowing students to work alone or with peers.

Process

As previously mentioned, Tomlinson defines process as the activities designed to ensure that students use key skills to make sense out of essential ideas and information. It is how students gain an understanding of the main idea(s) of the unit. It is how the student gains the information necessary to answer the essential questions of the unit. Some ways in which to differentiate process are

- tiered activities (a series of related tasks of varying complexity);
- learning contracts based on the readiness, interest, or learning profile of the student;
- independent learning/study;
- choice boards;
- acceleration/deceleration;
- flexible grouping;
- peer teaching;
- reading buddies; and
- learning centers.

Product

Products are one way in which to assess a student's knowledge and understanding of a topic. For some students, it is a much more comprehensive and rich way in which to demonstrate what they know. Tomlinson identified guidelines for successful product differentiation. Some ways in which to differentiate product are

- write a story or poem,
- write a book report,
- debate an issue,
- design a model or game,
- construct a model or game,
- investigate an issue,
- write a play,
- perform a play,
- compare and contrast, and
- create a mural or song.

In each of the above categories—*content*, *process*, and *product*—only a few examples were listed.

BLOOM'S TAXONOMY ■

Remember Bloom's taxonomy that was presented earlier in this chapter and in Chapters 2 and 5? Bloom theorized that learning is a process beginning with knowledge of the subject, comprehension of the material, application of the material, analysis of what is being taught, synthesis to make new ideas, and finally, evaluation of the content being learned. He believed that in any classroom, one would find students at each step of this process. Some would reach the evaluation step quite quickly while others would only reach the knowledge step.

Teachers who are trying to differentiate instruction can also use Bloom's taxonomy as a way to ensure that they are reaching *all* the students in their classrooms. Teachers are encouraged to design products that match with each step of the taxonomy. For example, using the schematic in Figure 6.6, one can see that debating an issue falls along the analysis step of Bloom's taxonomy while writing a book report would fall on the knowledge step.

It is important to note that there are many ways in which to differentiate instruction; we are not advocating any particular method. We simply are advocating that teachers design multiple ways to instruct students.

HOMEWORK

Another facet to differentiated instruction is homework. Several researchers support our idea. Harris Cooper (2001) has conducted the most extensive research to date on homework. He analyzed 17 studies involving 3,300 students in 85 classrooms and 30 schools in 11 states. He discovered that the average student completing homework had a higher achievement score than 55 percent of the students who did not complete homework.

Cooper offers several suggestions for teachers, administrators, and parents on how to make homework an effective teaching tool. Cooper views homework as a diagnostic tool rather than as an opportunity to test. Teachers must clearly state the purposes, types, and length of homework to students. Homework should have a clear purpose in mind, be geared to the developmental level of the child, and be reviewed by the teacher each day. Cooper theorizes that homework should focus on practice, integrations of concepts learned during the day, and simple introductions to the next lesson. Shorter and more frequent assignments are more effective for elementary school students.

Cooper also found that positive effects for homework did vary with the subject matter. The greatest positive effects were found in mathematics assignments, followed by reading, English, science, and social studies. Cooper does not believe in the grading of assignments, as he sees this as hampering the positive effects of developing good study habits. He also found that homework's effectiveness increases with the age of the child. It has its greatest effects on high school students.

He emphasizes that homework should *not* be busywork, punishment, or extra work because one finished early in class. These strategies will only cause more troubles down the road. If teachers use homework as punishment or busywork, they only reinforce the student's negativity about homework, a fact that may be inadvertently reinforced by the parents' own opinions about homework.

James Stronge (2002), in another research study, agrees with Cooper on the three basic purposes of homework: practice, preparation, and elaboration. Stronge also points out that high school students who spend an additional 30 minutes per night on homework may increase their grade point average by one half-point. If teachers are going to help students show improved academic scores later in their academic careers, we need to train elementary school children to complete homework each day.

The purposes for homework as described by Cooper and Stronge fit well with the concepts of differentiation by respecting a student's readiness and skill level to begin a particular homework assignment. Most of

Figure 6.6   A Sampling of Instructional Products Using Multiple Intelligences and Bloom's Taxonomy

	Verbal-Linguistic	Logical-Mathematical	Visual-Spatial	Musical-Rhythmic	Bodily-Kinesthetic	Naturalist	Interpersonal	Intrapersonal
Evaluation	Create a poem expressing the hazards of a pirate's life.	Rate three different nautical logs for accuracy of ships' positions.	Critique one of the pirate films seen in class.	Rate your favorite sea shanty and describe why.	Pretend you are a judge and act out how you would try to judge the pirate Greybeard.	Explain the effect of global warming on the Isles of Shoals.	Prepare a defense for a pirate in front of your peers.	Explain how your opinion has changed or stayed the same regarding pirates.
Synthesis	Explain how piracy supported various governments.	Given a beginning location and destination, trade winds, and supplies, project the length of a voyage.	Create a large mural using information learned about pirates.	Burn a CD containing sea shanties and sea songs.	Assemble a mobile depicting pirate life.	Organize a list of plant or wildlife that existed in the 17th century and is now extinct.	Summarize the relationship between a pirate ship captain and his crew.	Plan a field trip that would demonstrate what you learned in this unit.
Analysis	Compare the stories of Celia Thaxter as presented by Stephanie Voss with the storytelling of Brownie Macintosh.	Analyze a typical pirate's diet and identify deficiencies in vitamins and minerals.	Compare the traits of the main characters of the movies *The Black Pirate* and *Lethal Weapon*.	Classify shanties by historical period.	Create large clay models of pirates.	Categorize at least five sea animals by genus and species.	Debate the stereotype of a pirate's life vs. the facts.	Share your opinion of pirate life before and after this unit.
Application	Create a pirate ABC book.	Design a pirate ship model.	Design pirate clothing for a mannequin.	Perform a musical skit with two or three friends.	Construct a pirate ship model.	Investigate ecological issues on the Isles of Shoals.	Survey class to design a board game on piracy.	Write a letter to a loved one as a captive on a pirate ship.
Comprehension	Explain the horse latitudes and doldrums.	Convert a dollar into the value of a Spanish doubloon.	Sequence pictures of pirates and piracy into a story.	Demonstrate on drums various rhythms used by the men in the galley while rowing.	Identify flags of nations that existed in the 17th century.	Classify at least 10 plants found on the Isles of Shoals.	Report on the perception of your classmates regarding piracy.	Share your feelings regarding the Isles of Shoals experience.
Knowledge	Write a book report detailing the pirate facts learned.	Make a list of diseases sailors were subject to while at sea.	Collect pictures illustrating pirates.	Recite three sea shanties.	Label the sections of a galleon model.	Identify five bodies of water frequented by pirates.	Quote three pirates and survey peers for reaction to the quotes.	Recall the most interesting facts you learned from the speakers.

the suggestions listed under content, process, and product for classroom work can also be utilized for homework assignments. (An added benefit to using differentiated homework assignments is that it allows parents to experience firsthand what strategies you are using in the classroom!)

Naturally, one of the most important questions for parents is how long homework should be. Both the National Parent Teacher Association (Villaire, 2005) and the National Education Association have endorsed the following guidelines for the length of homework for elementary students: For children in Grades K–2, experts recommend no more than 10–20 minutes of homework each school day. Older children, in Grades 3–6, can handle 30–60 minutes a day. In junior and senior high school, the amount of homework will vary by subject. Older students may also have homework projects that could have deadlines that are weeks away. They may need help organizing assignments and planning work times to make sure homework is ready to turn in on time.

■ DIFFERENTIATION AND STANDARDS

Given that we have promoted the use of standards and are now suggesting lessons be differentiated by the needs of our students, you are probably wondering how to accomplish this. Most teachers make the assumption that using standards means cookie cutter lessons that are boring and solely focused on test results. Quite the contrary is true! Tomlinson (2000) addressed this issue. She states,

> There is no contradiction between effective standards-based instruction and differentiation. Curriculum tells us *what* to teach: Differentiation tells us *how*. Thus if we elect to teach a standards-based curriculum, differentiation simply suggests ways in which we can make that curriculum work best for varied learners. In other words, differentiation can show us how to teach the same standard to a range of learners by employing a variety of teaching and learning modes. (p. 4)

In summary, we recommend that teachers have a methodology to their lesson planning, be it mastery teaching, mastery learning, or a framework for teaching. We advise that they use research-based instructional strategies as described by Marzano, Pickering, and Pollock (2001). We strongly suggest that teachers incorporate essential questions into lesson deign and implementation. Finally, we hope that teachers will use strategies that differentiate instruction as well as homework, as proposed by Tomlinson, Bloom, and Cooper.

In our next chapter, we will show you how we put together all these ideas in a mapped, differentiated, interdisciplinary model.

7

Mapped, Differentiated, and Interdisciplinary Units

INTERDISCIPLINARY UNITS ■

What is interdisciplinary teaching? It is an approach that thoughtfully incorporates and connects key concepts and skills from many disciplines into the presentation of a single unit. Interdisciplinary teaching focuses on big ideas such as *freedom* or *organisms*, while requiring students to use the higher order thinking skills of Bloom's taxonomy (i.e., analysis, synthesis, and evaluation). To be clear, interdisciplinary teaching is not just a connection of facts across disciplines. It is a methodology to help students make connections.

Why would we advocate using interdisciplinary units? The answer is plain and simple: making connections! Recent studies of children's brains suggest that there is ample reason for teachers to use interdisciplinary teaching. Cells of the brain are called *neurons*, and they connect to one another in what are called *neuronal networks*. According to James Zull (2002), noted brain researcher, "The single most important factor in learning is the existing networks of neurons in the learners' brain. Ascertain what they are and teach accordingly" (p. 93).

Zull theorizes that the brain is constructed of bits of information that are located in small groups of neurons located in small groups of networks that are connected to other networks. In fact, the brain has *100 billion* neurons and there are estimates that each neuron has *10,000* connections. Thus we can recognize and write our name without really thinking, or connect a song to a movie or recall a memory in connection to that song. Given this, it is obvious that the brain thrives on connections. When we assist students by making the connections clearer, we are tapping into the innate strength of the brain!

In addition, H. Lynn Erickson (2002), curriculum developer and researcher, states,

> In this age of information overload, students need a mental schema to pattern and sort information. As they progress through the grades, students build conceptual structures in their brain as they relate new examples to past learnings. This means that teachers, in writing curricula, need to identify conceptual ideas, often stated as essential understandings, that are developmentally appropriate for the age level of their students. (p. 51)

So if connections are important, if understanding your students' learning styles and multiple intelligences are critical, and mapping your units to meet state and federal standards is of great value, then why not combine all three?

We were part of a great group of teachers who did just that. We would like to share with you two interdisciplinary units that were mapped and differentiated by multiple intelligences and learning style.

■ PIRATES

In the first unit, you shall see individual style differences in the way it was designed and presented. We truly respect the diversity of learners among the developers of the two example units and our readers. Each used different formats for planning to address their different learning styles. (As an aside, many teachers use technology to brainstorm ideas or to web thoughts. There are several exciting software programs available such as Inspiration, Mindmap, and Brainstorm. We are not promoting the use of any one of these programs, merely informing you, the reader, that software is available, relatively inexpensive, and great to use, especially when planning as a group.)

Our first example, a unit on pirates, was developed by a group of middle school teachers.

You will see in Figure 7.1 that the teachers identified a key concept, *fact or fiction,* by using the theme of pirates. After a series of meetings, we identified a purpose, a set of essential questions, and the skeleton of the content, process, and products we wanted to teach to the students. This healthy discussion required us to focus our energies on a cohesive whole rather than a core content-specific requirement.

Figure 7.1   Planning Document Developed by Sensing-Thinking Learner

Facts Versus Fiction: Pirates

Purpose: *Gain an understanding of the exploration to the New World in the 16th century*
Content: Interact simulation, *Galleon*
Process: Large- and small-group activities, plus individual activities
Product: Some of the activities were to draw a map, complete a research project, and complete the "journey" in the simulation.

Purpose: *Gain a greater understanding of the lives and surroundings of pirates.*
Content: Novels (*Buccaneers* by Ian Lawrence, *Captain Grey* by Avi, *Terror of the Spanish Main* by Albert Marrin, other fiction and nonfiction related to the topics of pirates and piracy)
Process: Read-alouds, individual reading, free read, literary circles, book discussions
Product: Students could select from 48 different possibilities.

Purpose: *Connect local history and places to pirates and piracy*
Content: Guest speakers:

1. A musician and author performed in full pirate regalia, taking students on a literary and musical journey down the East Coast and around Cape Horn and up to San Francisco. Students experienced traditional songs of the sea.
2. The Captain of the Isles of Shoals Steamship Company and marine historian shared stories about some of the people and events that make up the local history of the Isles. He also spoke about the various types of ships used in the area during the 1700s and navigation tools.
3. A local actress portrayed 19th-century poet and folklorist Celia Thaxter, sharing stories of pirates and shipwrecks.
4. Marine biologists brought small marine animals, such as a sea star and mussels, to the class for students to observe.

Process: Field trip to the Isles of Shoals on a Victorian steamship replica
Product: Some of the activities that were done in small groups and as individuals were (a) draw illustrations that depicted the tale of Blackbeard's bride; (b) identify famous Isles of Shoals landmarks and points of interest on a map that was provided; (c) locate where Captain Haley, the first citizen of the Shoals, found buried treasure; (d) draw and name one of the lighthouses they had seen (required in the drawing was some of the wildlife they had seen); (e) identify five sea animals and list each animal's characteristics; and (f) identify, list, and discuss some conservation issues for our local rivers and streams.

Purpose: *Fantasy vs. fact: What are the stereotypes of pirates as portrayed by the media? What is the media formula?*
Content: In a class of approximately 20 students, students viewed three films from different time periods (*Seahawk, The Black Pirate,* and *Captain Blood*).
Process: As a whole class or in small groups, students brainstormed a list of similar traits that described the main character of each movie; identified traits of the "hero" and of the "villain"; discussed and evaluated the list of traits; and compared these traits to other characters in movies, such as *Lethal Weapon,* based on these traits.
Product: Students developed a presentation illustrating a character, and discussed and summarized what are the stereotypes of pirates and what is the media formula for the development of a hero and antihero.

In Figure 7.2, we developed a detailed curriculum map of the performance standards, essential questions, content, skills, and assessments that we intended to use. We also added a list of resources and technology useful to the unit.

Figure 7.2   Pirates: Grade 6 Interdisciplinary Unit

Local Performance Standards	*Language Arts*: Students will be able to research by reading multiple sources (including print and nonprint texts) to report information, to solve a problem, to make a decision, or to formulate a judgment. Students will be able to analyze and interpret elements of literary texts, citing evidence where appropriate by describing characters' traits, motivations, or interactions, citing thoughts, words, or actions that reveal characters' traits, motivations, or changes over time. *Math*: Students will be able to measure and use units of measurement appropriately and consistently and make conversions within systems when solving problems across the content strands. Students will be able to make estimates in a given situation by identifying when estimation is appropriate, selecting the appropriate method of estimation, determining the level of accuracy needed in a given situation, analyzing the effect of the estimation method on the accuracy of the results, and evaluating the reasonableness of the solutions. *Science*: Students will be able to demonstrate an increasing ability to understand how environmental factors affect all living systems as well as species-to-species interactions by tracing the interactions between man and the environment that demonstrate how human activities can deliberately or inadvertently alter the equilibrium of an ecosystem. *Social Studies*: Students will be able to explain the unique contributions of different ethnic and religious groups to New Hampshire history and culture, such as, but not limited to, the Shakers or the French Canadians. Students will be able to describe the impact of land and water routes on trade such as, but not limited to, the Silk Roads, the Atlantic Triangle of Trade, or the Suez Canal.
Content/Theme	Pirates
Essential Questions	✓ What is fact and what is fiction regarding the behaviors and lives of pirates? ✓ How have pirates/piracy impacted local histories? ✓ Do pirates exist today? ✓ Is piracy for a cause morally justified?
Skills	✓ Create poems, critiques, films, books, murals, mobiles, and opinions regarding pirates' lives. ✓ Analyze and rate three different nautical logs for accuracy of ships' positions. ✓ Debate and defend a pirate's actions. ✓ Compare and contrast differing versions of piracy, discovering what is real and what is fantasy. ✓ Know parts of a ship and types of ships. ✓ Analyze and explain the effects of global warming on the Isles of Shoals, and plant or wildlife that existed in the 17th century and is now extinct. ✓ Research life on a pirate ship, including diet. ✓ Predict the length of a voyage given a beginning location and destination, trade winds, and supplies. ✓ Know the traits and characteristics of a pirate of the 17th century versus those in the twenty-first century. ✓ Classify shanties by historical period.
Assessment/ Products	✓ Pretest of existing knowledge ✓ Presentation choices as rated by rubric ✓ Teacher observations ✓ Teacher-prepared quizzes or tests
Resources	✓ Artists in residence or guest artists to perform the stories of Celia Thaxter ✓ Local newspapers ✓ Books: *Captain Grey* by Avi (1993); *The Buccaneers* by I. Lawrence (2003); *Pirates!* by C. Rees (2003); *Treasure Island* (Scribner Classics) by R. Louis Stevenson (1981); *The Mystery of Blackbeard the Pirate* by C. Marsh (2003); *Mystery at Blackbeard's Cove* by A. Penn (2004)
Technology	✓ PowerPoint software ✓ Midi and musical composition software ✓ Movies: *Lethal Weapon*, *Pirates of the Caribbean*, and *The Black Pirate* ✓ National Geographic: http://www.nationalgeographic.com/expeditions/atlas/ ✓ Preserving the remains of Blackbeard's flagship: http://www.ah.dcr.state. nc.us/qar/ ✓ Pirate ship Whydah: http://www.nationalgeographic.com/whydah/story.html ✓ Isles of Shoals: http://seacoastnh.com/shoals/history.html

As part of the unit, students self-selected from a group of novels on the theme of pirates. These books spanned a wide range of reading and topic areas. As a demonstration of their knowledge gained from reading the books, students were given a choice of assessment product. Some of the choices in Figure 7.3 were teacher generated, while others were student generated.

Figure 7.3   Presentation Choices, Pirates Unit

Presentation Choices: Based on the book they read, students must create a presentation from among the following choices.

1.   Create a poem expressing the hazards of a pirate's life.
2.   Rate three different nautical logs for accuracy of ships' positions.
3.   Critique one of the pirate films seen in class.
4.   Rate your favorite sea shanty and describe why.
5.   Pretend you are a judge and act out how you would try to judge the pirate Greybeard.
6.   Explain the effects of global warming on the Isles of Shoals.
7.   Prepare a defense for a pirate in front of your peers.
8.   Explain how your opinion has changed or stayed the same regarding pirates.
9.   Explain how piracy supported various governments.
10. Given a beginning location and destination, trade winds, and supplies, project the length of a voyage.
11. Create a large mural using information learned about pirates.
12. Burn a CD containing sea shanties and sea songs.
13. Assemble a mobile depicting pirate life.
14. Organize a list of plant or wildlife that existed in the 17th century and is now extinct.
15. Summarize the relationship between a pirate ship captain and his crew.
16. Plan a field trip that would demonstrate what you have learned in this unit.
17. Compare the stories of Celia Thaxter as presented by Stephanie Voss with the storytelling of Brownie Macintosh.
18. Analyze a typical pirate's diet and identify deficiencies in vitamins and minerals.
19. Compare the traits of the main characters of the movies *The Black Pirate* and *Lethal Weapon*.
20. Classify shanties by historical period.
21. Create large clay models of pirates.
22. Categorize at least five sea animals by genus and species.
23. Debate the stereotype of a pirate's life versus the facts.
24. Share your opinion of pirate life before and after this unit.
25. Create a pirate ABC book.
26. Design a pirate ship model.
27. Design pirate clothing for a mannequin.
28. Perform a musical skit with two or three friends.
29. Construct a pirate ship model.
30. Investigate ecological issues on the Isles of Shoals.
31. Survey the class to design a board game on piracy.
32. Write a letter to a loved one as a captive on a pirate ship.
33. Explain the horse latitudes and doldrums.
34. Convert a dollar into the value of a Spanish doubloon.
35. Sequence pictures of pirates and piracy into a story.
36. Demonstrate on drums various rhythms used by the men in the galley while rowing.
37. Identify flags of nations that existed in the 17th century.
38. Classify at least 10 plants found on the Isles of Shoals.
39. Report on the perception of your classmates regarding piracy.
40. Share your feelings regarding your Isles of Shoals experience.
41. Make a chart of pirate facts learned.
42. Make a list of diseases sailors were subject to while at sea.
43. Collect pictures illustrating pirates.
44. Recite three sea shanties.
45. Label the sections of a galleon model.
46. Identify five bodies of water frequented by pirates.
47. Quote three pirates and survey peers for reactions to the quotes.
48. Recall the most interesting facts you learned from one of the speakers.

Teachers designed a rubric for use with the students. We reviewed the rubric with the students, ensuring that they understood it, a practice reinforcing literacy as well as discipline-specific expectations. We did not assume that all students would comprehend the written instructions. This rubric is illustrated in Figure 7.4.

This amazingly successful unit has been repeated for three years now and is still evolving as the teachers and students add new ideas every year.

As you can see, these research-based documents and strategies can become the foundation of your teaching. The rest is left up to your art as a teacher.

■ BRIDGES

A fourth grade teacher, Carolyn Clithero, developed our second example, a unit on bridges. We expanded upon that unit to illustrate our model. We used a graphic organizer to develop our ideas. In Figure 7.5, you can see all the content areas and essential questions we hoped to cover.

As with the pirate unit, we created a curriculum map, which indicated the performance standards we are addressing, along with the content, skills, and assessments. We found a wealth of materials online and in libraries to help with this unit.

Since this unit is designed for younger students, we limited the number of choices to 12 and included activities to fit multiple intelligences and Bloom's taxonomy.

Figure 7.4   Rubric for Pirates Unit

	1	2	3	4
Effort/Personal Best	This work lacks effort. This needs work.	Your work shows moderate effort. You are capable of much more.	You did all that I asked you to. You could have stretched a bit more.	This is *your* best work! I don't think you could have done better. Awesome!
Presentation	Very messy. Quality is poor.	Parts are messy. Parts lack quality.	Neat. High quality.	Superbly done. Exemplary (I'd use this as a sample).
Completeness	Many parts are missing.	You are missing parts of the required tasks.	All tasks required are completed.	All tasks required are completed with extra details and/ or additional work.
Accuracy and Quality of Thought	Information is incorrect or missing. Misinterpreted or lacks understanding of the subject.	Basic thinking. Some inaccuracies or misconceptions.	Critical thinking is beginning. Applies understanding of the subject matter.	Evidence of critical thinking. Sophisticated application of the subject.

Figure 7.5   Planning Document for Bridge Unit as Developed by Sensing-Feeling
Learner

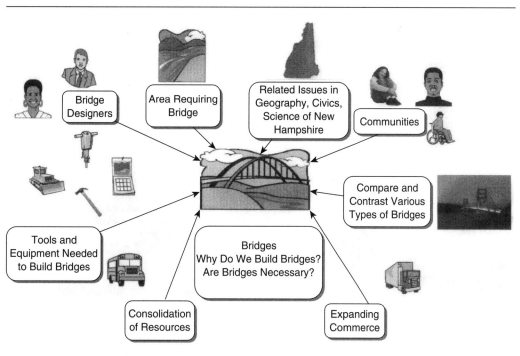

SOURCE: Diagram created in Inspiration® by Inspiration Software®, Inc.

Figure 7.6   Bridges: Grade 4 Interdisciplinary Unit

Performance Standard	*Language Arts*: Students will demonstrate initial understanding of informational texts (expository and practical texts) by obtaining information from text features (e.g., maps, diagrams, tables, captions, time lines).
	Students show breadth of vocabulary knowledge through demonstrating understanding of word meaning or relationships by identifying synonyms, antonyms, homonyms/homophones, or shades of meaning.
	Math: Students will use properties or attributes of angles or sides to identify, describe, or distinguish among triangles, squares, rectangles, rhombi, trapezoids, hexagons, or octagons, or classify angles relative to 90 degrees as more than, less than, or equal to.
	Science: Students will use appropriate tools and techniques to gather, organize, and interpret data.
	Students will demonstrate an increasing ability to understand that science and technology can affect individuals, and that individuals in turn can affect science and technology.
	Students will understand the meaning of models, their appropriate use and limitations, and how models can help them in understanding the natural world.
	Social Studies: Students will illustrate the ways in which regions change, such as, but not limited to, changes in local neighborhoods or changes to the United States through westward expansion.

(Continued)

Figure 7.6 (Continued)

Content/Theme	Bridges
Essential Question	✓ Why do we build bridges? ✓ Are bridges necessary?
Skills	✓ Research information using library, informational text, and the Internet. ✓ Read maps for characteristics of surrounding areas. ✓ Identify angles in the seven bridges from pictures. ✓ List characteristics of the various types of bridges. ✓ Take notes while viewing a video on bridges. ✓ Construct a graph. ✓ Analyze the effects of bridges on the development of communities. ✓ Design and label a bridge made out of balsa wood. ✓ Describe various meanings of the word *bridge* (i.e., bridge of a ship; bridge, the card game; bridge of a musical instrument; bridge as in dentures).
Assessment/ Products	✓ Pretest of existing knowledge ✓ Diary of mathematical steps in bridge construction ✓ Student's record and definition of associated vocabulary ✓ Completion of the writing prompt ✓ Completion of writing essays ✓ PowerPoint presentation or video ✓ Construction of model bridge with proper use of geometric terms ✓ Performance of a skit or play about a bridge's construction ✓ Performance of debate or oral presentations ✓ Composition of a song about bridges and description of its meaning ✓ Observations made by teacher
Resources	✓ Adkins, J. (2002), *Bridges: From My Side to Yours* ✓ Carter, P. (1992), *The Bridge Book* ✓ Doyle, B. (1990), *Covered Bridge* ✓ Galdone, P. (1981), *Three Billy Goats Gruff* ✓ Johmann, C. (1999), *Bridges: Amazing Structures to Design, Build & Test* ✓ Kaner, E. (1995), *Bridges* ✓ Mann, E. and Witschonke, A. (1996), *The Brooklyn Bridge: A Wonders of the World Book* ✓ Paterson, K. (1987), *Bridge to Terabithia* ✓ Petroski, H. (1996), *Engineers of Dreams: Great Bridge Builders and the Spanning of America* ✓ Scieszka, J. (2002), *Hey Kid, Want to Buy a Bridge?* ✓ Sturges, P. (1998), *Bridges Are to Cross* ✓ Swift, H., and Ward, L. (2002), *The Little Red Lighthouse and the Great Gray Bridge* ✓ Weatherford, C. (2002), *Remember the Bridge: Poems of a People* ✓ Winters, J. (2005), *Mystic Uncle and the Magical Bridge*
Technology	✓ Big Dig Web site: http://www.masspike.com/bigdig/index.html ✓ Burns, K. (2003), *Brooklyn Bridge*, PBS Home Video DVD ✓ Leonard P. Zakim Bunker Hill Bridge Web site: http://www.leonardpzakimbunkerhillbridge.org/ ✓ Macauley, D., *Building Big: Bridges*, WGBH Boston, VHS or DVD ✓ Macauley, D., Building Big: Bridges Web site: http://www.pbs.org/wgbh/buildingbig/bridge/index.html ✓ New Hampshire Covered Bridges: http://www.state.nh.us/nhdhr/bridges/ ✓ Physics Balsa Bridge Building Contest online: http://www.balsabridge.com/

Figure 7.7   Bridges Product Choices

Directions: Read each of the choices below carefully. Join another student to read the directions again to see if you both understand them correctly.

Each student must finish numbers 1–8. You will be given class time each day to work on these.

You then must choose one assignment from numbers 9–12 to complete. Choose the item that you really *like* doing. You will do this assignment for homework.

ALL STUDENTS MUST FINISH ITEMS 1–8.

1. Listen to our guest engineer. Take notes in your bridge journal on the seven types of bridges we will be studying: *arch bridges* (Bayonne Bridge in New York), *beam bridges* (Chesapeake Bridge in Maryland), *cable stay bridges* (Leonard Zakim Bridge in Boston), *covered bridges* (Cornish Windsor Covered Bridge in New Hampshire), *drawbridges* (Memorial Bridge in Maine), *truss bridges* (Old General Sullivan Bridge in New Hampshire), and *suspension bridges* (Golden Gate Bridge in California).
2. Pick four partners and see how many of the bridge types you can make just using your bodies. Write down the types you were able to make.
3. Find each bridge on a state map and mark it. Choose one bridge and draw a picture of what you think the area around the bridge looked like before the bridge was built.
4. Write an essay about the bridge area that you drew. Describe the type of waterway that the bridge crosses. Describe what kinds of businesses were there before the bridge was built. Write about the businesses that you would expect to see around the bridge now. Explain how plants have changed and how animals around the bridge area have moved away.
5. Research two of the major bridge construction projects we studied: the Bayonne Bridge in New York, the Chesapeake Bridge in Maryland, the Zakim Bridge in Massachusetts (the Big Dig), the Cornish Windsor Covered Bridge in New Hampshire, the Memorial Bridge in Maine, the Old General Sullivan Bridge in New Hampshire, and the Golden Gate Bridge in California.

   ✓ Create a portfolio that contains pictures of both bridges; the names of the architect-engineers; and the type, height, length, cost, and time of construction of each bridge.
   ✓ Graph the type, height, length, cost, and time of construction of each bridge.
   ✓ Think about the reasons why the bridges were built and record your guesses. Check your hypotheses with your research. List your guesses and what you discovered.
   ✓ Pick a partner to make either a PowerPoint presentation or a video of your research on the two bridges. Be sure to include 10 historical facts about the bridges and their surrounding communities. Compare and contrast what is the same and what is different about each bridge and its community.

6. Build a model bridge out of balsa wood. Label your design with the geometric terms we studied: right angle, acute angle, obtuse angle, and line segment.
7. Read *one* book about bridges. Chose either *Bridge to Terabithia*, by K. Paterson; *Hey Kid, Want to Buy a Bridge?* by J. Scieszka; *The Little Red Lighthouse and the Great Gray Bridge*, by H. Swift and L. Ward; *Mystic Uncle and the Magical Bridge*, by J. Winters; or *Remember the Bridge: Poems of a People*, by C. Weatherford. Write a one-page report on the meaning of the word *bridge* in the book you chose.
8. Write a song to the prompt "If I cross this bridge . . . ."

Choose one assignment from this group for homework.

9. Sing your song about bridges for the class. Tell how you felt when you were writing and singing it.
10. Choose a friend for a debate. Debate in front of the class which type of bridge you think is better and why.
11. Create and perform a short play about someone who is building a bridge and why he or she is building it.
12. Draw a picture book about the plants and animals that live around bridges. Show how the animals were affected by the bridge's construction. Explain the book to the class.

As in the pirates unit (shown in Figure 5.2), we developed a chart to differentiate products on bridges. Here are other possibilities you could use with your class.

Figure 7.8 A Sampling of Other Instructional Products Using Multiple Intelligences and Bloom's Taxonomy

	Verbal-Linguistic	Logical-Mathematical	Visual-Spatial	Musical-Rhythmic	Bodily-Kinesthetic	Naturalist	Interpersonal	Intrapersonal
Evaluation	Give a speech on Mr. Leonard Zakim. Explain why the bridge was named for him.	Compare three bridge designs and estimate which type would cost the most to build.	Review two Road Runner cartoons that have bridges in them. Explain whether these bridges would really work.	Listen to the song "Bridge Over Troubled Water." Explain in writing what the term *bridge* means in the title.	Make up a skit in which you are a bridge builder. Defend your choice of bridge type to the mayor.	Explain the effects of global warming on major bridges throughout the U.S.	Prepare a list of various uses of bridges during wartime. Debate these with a friend who does not agree with war.	Write an essay explaining how your thinking about bridges has changed.
Synthesis	Pretend you are a state park ranger. Explain how the Golden Gate Bridge was built.	Given the size and type of model bridge, figure the materials needed and length of construction.	Give a speech showing the strengths and weaknesses of each type of bridge. Use models or pictures if possible.	Compare and contrast the London Bridge nursery rhyme with the real London Bridge. Why do you think the song was written?	Create a drawing showing the soil layers needed to build a bridge.	Compare the bridges made by animals to those made by man.	Explain the relationship between an architect, engineers, and the construction crew.	Choose a bridge-building job that appeals to you and describe why.
Analysis	Compare the challenges of bridge builders W. Roebling and Joseph Strauss.	Graph and explain the numbers of resources needed to build two different bridges.	Using maps, compare the reasons two communities decided to build a bridge.	Write a report on how music bridges gaps between countries.	Build a suspension bridge using the materials in the classroom.	Compare what metals used in bridge building will endanger water animals.	Debate the benefits and dangers of being a bridge builder.	Write an essay describing which bridge design appeals to you the most.
Application	Choose a river near your home and write a report on what type of bridge design would be best and why.	Design a bridge model using the geometric angles we studied in class.	Take photos of a bridge and explain how each part works.	Write a song about covered bridges.	Build one type of bridge model using balsa wood.	Research the ecological issues of bridge construction.	Ask the class for their opinions about General John Sullivan, for whom the N.H. bridge is named.	Write a poem about a child's feelings watching a bridge being built.
Comprehension	Explain three types of bridges and under what land forms each is best.	Identify the types of angles used in making bridges.	Draw a painting showing various persons and vehicles using a bridge. Explain their purpose in using the bridge.	Research songs about bridges and describe the multiple meanings of the word *bridge*.	Form bridges using hands, arms, and feet and explain how each section works.	Describe what natural conditions are improved through building bridges.	Tell the class the effects of bridges on local towns.	Write a story of your own experiences with bridges.
Knowledge	Make a chart of bridge facts learned.	Make a list of bridges in several major cities.	Collect pictures showing different types of bridges.	Recite or sing two songs involving bridges.	Label the sections of a bridge.	Find five bodies of water in the U.S. that have bridges.	Read *Three Billy Goats Gruff* and survey your friends about their fears about bridges.	Recall the most interesting facts you learned from one of the guest speakers.

Figure 7.9 Rubric for Bridge Unit

Trait	4	3	2	1
Comprehends the ways in which regions change through the use of technology. Uses new vocabulary regarding bridges and shows shades of meanings for the word _bridge_.	✓ You know all the bridge types we studied. ✓ You always know what bridge type is best for different waterways. ✓ You fully describe how areas around bridges change and how those changes affect plants and animals. ✓ You write five different sentences showing the many meanings of the word _bridge_.	✓ You know most of the bridge types we studied. ✓ You mostly know what bridge type is best for different waterways. ✓ You partially describe how areas around bridges change and how those changes affect plants and animals. ✓ You write three different sentences showing the many meanings of the word _bridge_.	✓ You know some of the bridge types we studied. ✓ You sometimes know what bridge type is best for different waterways. ✓ You sometimes describe how areas around bridges change and how those changes affect plants and animals. ✓ You write one sentence showing the many meanings of the word _bridge_.	✓ You need more help in learning the bridge types we studied. ✓ You do not know what bridge type is best for different waterways. ✓ You need more help in describing how areas around bridges change and how those changes affect plants and animals. ✓ You cannot write any sentences showing the many meanings of the word _bridge_.
Demonstrates understanding of the use of models. Builds bridge using proper angles and correct math operations.	✓ You identify the type of bridge from each of the class models all the time. ✓ You correctly name all the angles used in your bridge construction. ✓ While building your bridge model, you choose the right math operation and correctly figure out the problem all the time.	✓ You identify the type of bridge from each of the class models most of the time. ✓ You correctly name most of the angles used in your bridge construction. ✓ While building your bridge model, you choose the right math operation and correctly figure out the problem most of the time.	✓ You identify the type of bridge from each of the class models some of the time. ✓ You correctly name some of the angles used in your bridge construction. ✓ While building your bridge model, you choose the right math operation and correctly figure out the problem some of the time.	✓ You identify one or two of the types of bridge from each of the class models. ✓ You correctly name only one of the angles used in your bridge construction. ✓ While building your bridge model, you rarely choose the right math operation and correctly figure out the problem.
Obtains information from maps and graphs. Uses appropriate tools to gather information, organize it, and interpret it.	✓ In your project, you correctly research and organize information from maps, books, and other sources on bridges all the time. ✓ In your project, you correctly graph and interpret data all the time.	✓ In your project, you correctly research and organize information from maps, books, and other sources on bridges most of the time. ✓ In your project, you correctly graph and interpret data most of the time.	✓ In your project, you correctly research and organize information from maps, books, and other sources on bridges some of the time. ✓ In your project, you correctly graph and interpret data some of the time.	✓ In your project, you rarely research and organize information from maps, books, and other sources on bridges. ✓ In your project, you rarely graph and interpret data.
Analyzes the historical, social, and economic effects of bridges.	✓ You describe 10 historical facts about the bridges you chose to study and why they are important. ✓ You compare and contrast five effects of your bridges on the communities surrounding them.	✓ You describe seven historical facts about the bridges that you chose to study and why they are important. ✓ You compare and contrast three effects of your bridges on the communities surrounding them.	✓ You describe four historical facts about the bridges that you chose to study and why they are important. ✓ You compare and contrast one effect of your bridges on the communities surrounding them.	✓ You describe one historical fact about the bridges you chose to study and why it is important. ✓ You do not compare and contrast effects of your bridges on the communities surrounding them.

Finally, we developed a rubric that specifically identifies the traits we are judging and gives the student the scope of what skills we are examining when assigning grades to their presentations (see Figure 7.9).

■ WHY USE THIS BLENDED APPROACH?

There are many reasons for using this blended approach. First, this blended model allows you to use many of the best research-based practices available while ensuring that you will meet all accountability requirements. In essence, we have combed the research for you and gathered the salient features into what we hope has been a coherent model.

Second, practically speaking, it is solid investment of a teacher's time. Each unit took approximately five hours of careful planning. However, these plans laid the groundwork for eight weeks of teaching and learning. In a nutshell, we

- determined which standards we needed to teach;
- mapped our curriculum to meet those standards;
- used a common theme to address multiple disciplines, thereby making those necessary connections for learners' brains;
- differentiated instruction according to our learners' needs and learning styles;
- designed a menu of product choices that took into account multiple intelligences; and
- held students accountable by using a consistent framework, rubrics, for judging their work.

Obviously, we used technology (and strongly encourage you to do so as well) to complete our work, but you can complete the templates we have provided for you in Chapter 8 with just paper and pencil.

Third, while the initial investment of time may be hard for any one teacher to find, the process is definitely enhanced if you can plan with a coteacher or a team. This is *not* a situation where too many cooks spoil the broth! In addition, these plans can be refined and reused the next year.

Fourth, through the use of these approaches, students will benefit by taking ownership of their learning. They will make connections by having multiple ways to gain knowledge. Students can demonstrate what they have learned at a level that challenges them. In addition, they have the opportunity to work in a variety of configurations, that is, individual, pair, small group, or large group.

Similarly, if we look at teachers as lifelong learners, they will have the benefit of discovering new insights regarding the pedagogy of teaching, the sharing of responsibility of student learning with the students themselves, and the expansion of their lessons resulting from the interests and perspectives of the other teachers and students.

8

Teachers' Tool Chests

Maryellen's Commitment

After reading through several books and talking with trusted friends, Maryellen has been able to choose strategies that work for her class. She has found that curriculum mapping is her best tool for organizing instruction. It has helped her plan more appropriately by relating instruction to state standards. By including essential questions in her maps, she has been able to hook children into the units no matter what their level of mastery. Differentiating instruction, once a difficult task, has become easier now that she is using multiple intelligence theory and Bloom's taxonomy and including differentiated products in her maps. Finally, she has joined other teachers, especially those in music, art, and physical education, to enhance the lessons she is teaching in the four content areas. By doing so, she has been able to reach those children for whom reading, writing, and math are very difficult.

What once seemed daunting is now manageable for Maryellen since she has chunked the information and set goals for herself. She has decided that she is going to try one new mapped, differentiated, interdisciplinary unit per quarter. She knows that with time, her repertoire of these lessons will grow. In addition, with research backing up her instructional decisions, she now addresses parents' concerns with more confidence.

Interestingly, the other teachers in third grade have expressed interest in joining with Maryellen. Little did she know when she started this project that she would become a pioneer. In helping others, she has found that these professional discussions have improved her lesson designs and instructional strategies. Even her principal is interested. She has been asked to share her strategies at a faculty meeting.

Patricia Wolfe (2001), in her book *Brain Matters: Translating Research in Classroom Practice*, said, "Being able to see how information fits together in chunks is, therefore, a hallmark of learning, a way of working with larger and larger amounts of information" (p. 99).

We have tried to chunk information while making connections for you, the reader, among the wide variety of research data available today. We have tried to practice what we preach by chunking information and by

✓ showing you the connections between national and state legislative initiatives, and local communities' demand for accountability;

✓ providing you with an instructional foundation combining a student-centered classroom with Bloom's taxonomy and metacognitive strategies;

✓ outlining the benefits of using curriculum mapping, whether you are in a group or alone;

✓ showing you ways to incorporate state and national standards and performance standards into units or themes;

✓ providing you with samples of assessment rubrics;

✓ illustrating how to incorporate multiple intelligences theory and learning styles into your design of instructional products;

✓ utilizing differentiated instruction to assist students by offering multiple formats for content, process, and products; and

✓ blending a student-centered environment with curriculum mapping, state and local standards, rubrics, multiple intelligences and learning styles, differentiated instruction, and interdisciplinary units into a cohesive model.

Since we do not know your set of prior knowledge, learning style, or multiple intelligences, we realize that you will need to make these connections for yourself in a way that makes sense to you. To assist you, we have provided blank models for you to use in assimilating this information.

In the next several pages, we have provided you with a blank graphic organizer for brainstorming ideas for new units. We have given you blank curriculum maps in three formats, basic, intermediate, and complex, for you to list your content, skills, and assessments. We have included a list of several free online learning style assessments for you and possibly your students to take. We have designed a blank matrix for you to create products by using multiple intelligences, Bloom's taxonomy, and learning styles. In addition, we have given you examples of student task cards that illustrate the use of Bloom's taxonomy with multiple intelligences theory and rubrics.

As we stated in the preface, we hoped this book would be your "tipping point." We hope that by seeing the connections among the wide breadth of new knowledge about the brain, the ways in which students learn, and the planning needed to ensure consistent exposure to required curricula, you will experience the excitement of contagiousness. We hope you experience how little changes can have big effects. We wish you the aha! dramatic moment when everything changes all at once.

Figure 8.1 Graphic Organizer for Blending Models

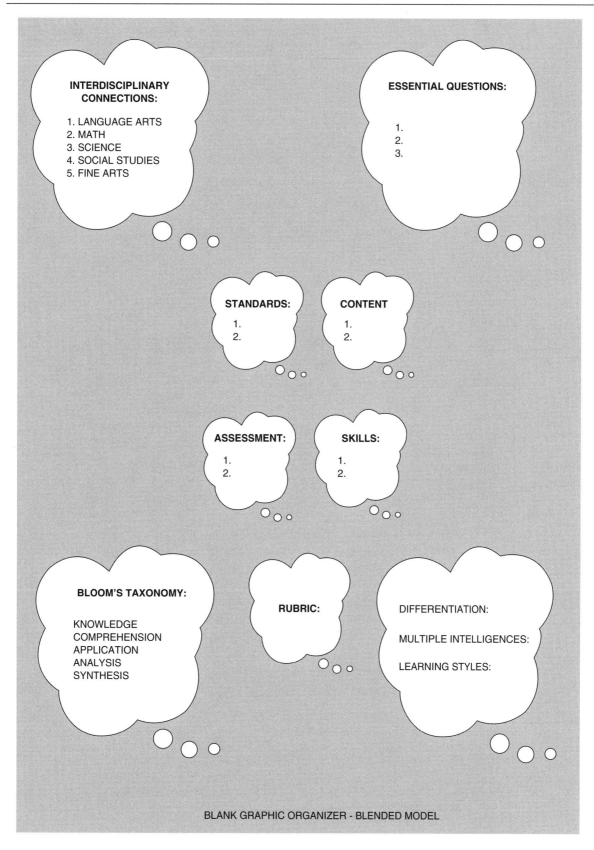

BLANK GRAPHIC ORGANIZER - BLENDED MODEL

SOURCE: Diagram created in Inspiration® by Inspiration Software®, Inc.

Figure 8.2   Blank Curriculum Map—Basic Format

	September	October	November
Content			
Skills			
Assessment/Products			

Figure 8.3   Blank Curriculum Map—Intermediate Format

	September	October	November
State/Local Curriculum Standards			
State/Local Performance Standards			
Content			
Skills			
Assessment/Products			

Figure 8.4 Blank Curriculum Map—Complex Format

	September	October	November
State/Local Curriculum Standards			
State/Local Performance Standards			
Essential Question			
Content			
Skills			
Assessment/Products			
Resources			
Technology			

Figure 8.5 Free Online Learning Style Assessments

Support4Learning Web Site
http://www.support4learning.org.uk/sites/support4learning/
education/learning_styles.cfm

Abiator's Online Learning Styles Inventory
http://www.berghuis.co.nz/abiator/lsi/lsiframe.html

Walter McKenzie's Surfaquarium: Multiple Intelligence in Education
http://surfaquarium.com/MI/

Thirteen Ed Online Concept to Classroom
http://www.thirteen.org/edonline/concept2class/mi/index.html

Figure 8.6 Instructional Products Using Multiple Intelligences, Bloom's Taxonomy, and Learning Styles

	Verbal-Linguistic	Logical-Mathematical	Visual-Spatial	Musical-Rhythmic	Bodily-Kinesthetic	Naturalist	Interpersonal	Intrapersonal
Evaluation	☐	☐	☐	☐	☐	☐	☐	☐
Synthesis	☐	☐	☐	☐	☐	☐	☐	☐
Analysis	☐	☐	☐	☐	☐	☐	☐	☐
Application	☐	☐	☐	☐	☐	☐	☐	☐
Comprehension	☐	☐	☐	☐	☐	☐	☐	☐
Knowledge	☐	☐	☐	☐	☐	☐	☐	☐

Copyright © 2007 by Corwin Press. All rights reserved. Reprinted from *Curriculum Mapping for Differentiated Instruction, K–8*, by Michelle A. Langa and Janice L. Yost. Thousand Oaks, CA: Corwin Press, www.corwinpress.com. Reproduction authorized only for the local school site or nonprofit organization that has purchased this book.

Figure 8.7   Pirate Project Choices

	Simple Projects in this column can be done in a shorter time frame. Work for 10 points.	Moderate Projects in this column take a bit more effort, planning, and time to complete. Work for 20 points.	Complex Projects in this column take a good amount of preplanning and time to complete. Work for 30 points.
Knowledge Know the basic facts	**Research** a nonfiction book about pirates. Share main ideas and details.	**List/Order** a time line of pirate events.	**Memorize** and give an oral interpretation of a part of a pirate novel or recitation of poetry involving pirate theme.
Comprehension Understand the facts	**Identify** the poster of the natural resources used by pirates, privateers, and shipbuilders.	**Classify/Identify** types of ships used by pirates, privateers, and others.	**Select** an ABC book using words associated with pirates and privateers.
Application Try your knowledge in a new area	**Illustrate** a favorite part of the novel *The Black Pirate*.	**Construct** a mobile of Isles of Shoals.	**Teach** an instrumental or vocal performance of a song related to piracy.
Analysis Analyze and make sense of the information	**Compare** a cartoon (two-panel) fantasy pirate to a real pirate.	**Categorize** A diorama of the sea life found along the coast of New Hampshire and the Isles of Shoals.	**Analyze** Design and write the front page of a pirate newspaper.
Evaluation Judge and evaluate info	**Assess/Judge** Write a review of a pirate film.	**Appraise** the symbolism on various Jolly Roger flags.	**Evaluate** A PowerPoint presentation on how all forms of media portray pirates.
Synthesis Put the facts into new structure/ format	**Draw** Become a captain of a ship and chart the course your ship would travel.	**Create** a scrapbook of a famous female pirate or privateer.	**Produce** a nine-panel comic strip on the life of a privateer or buccaneer.

Figure 8.8   Analyze Task Card

Task Card—Analyze (complex/analysis):
Pirate Newspaper Front Page

1. Collect the front pages of three different newspapers (for example, *Portsmouth Herald*, *Fosters Daily Democrat*, *Boston Globe*, *Hampton Union*).

   Check in with teacher. Teacher signature: _____

2. List *10* things that each of the front pages has in common.

   Check in with teacher. Teacher signature: _____

3. Using IIM and three documented resources, collect at least 30 note facts on a variety of pirate-related events and personalities that would be newsworthy (of interest, shocking, comical, or would have an impact on government or economy, etc.).

   Check in with teacher. Teacher signature: _____

4. Write six short articles based on your research and your own interpretations of the events.

   Check in with teacher. Teacher signature: _____

5. On a piece of 18″ × 24″ paper, create a front page of a newspaper. Include the items from Item 2, your six articles, and your works cited.

   Check in with teacher. Teacher signature: _____

Points: 30

	1	2	3	4
Effort/Personal Best	This work lacks effort. This needs work.	Your work shows moderate effort. You are capable of much more.	You did all that I asked you to. You could have stretched a bit more.	This is <u>your</u> best work! I don't think you could have done better. Awesome!
Presentation	Very messy. Quality is poor.	Parts are messy. Parts lack quality.	Neat. High quality.	Superbly done. Exemplary (I'd use this as a sample).
Completeness	Many parts are missing.	You are missing parts of the required tasks.	All tasks required are completed.	All tasks required are completed with extra details and/or additional work.
Accuracy and Quality of Thought	Information is incorrect or missing. Misinterpreted or lacks understanding of the subject.	Basic thinking. Some inaccuracies or misconceptions.	Critical thinking is beginning. Applies understanding of the subject matter.	Evidence of critical thinking. Sophisticated application of the subject.

SOURCE: Created by RJH teachers: K. Collyer, M. Coombs, M. Downer, J. Forrest, and J. Reese. Reprinted with permission from the Rye (NH) School Board.

Figure 8.9   Appraise Task Card

Task Card—Appraise (moderate/evaluation): Jolly Roger Flag Design

1. See Mr. Forrest for three handouts on the Jolly Roger flags.

2. Collect 25 different general note facts about the origin, history, and symbolism of the Jolly Roger flag.
   a. Collect five different specific note facts on each of the following *three* pirates and their flags:
      i. John Avery (also called Henry Every and Long Ben)
      ii. Captain Edward England
      iii. Calico Jack Rackham
   b. Choose *two* other pirates, and collect five different specific note facts about each of the pirates and their flags.

Check in with teacher. Teacher signature: _____

3. Using the Internet, visit the Web site listed at the bottom of the Google handout. Click on the Flags of Famous Pirates. Then, click on the names of the *five* pirates that you studied in Item 2. Print out their flags. Then, neatly trace, draw, or use construction paper to make the five flags.

4. When you appraise or evaluate something, you think about the quality or value or merit of that thing. You are a judge making a judgment of something's worth or importance. Now that you have had the opportunity to study several Jolly Roger flags and the stories attached to them, decide what is required for a quality design for that kind of flag.

5. Plan and make your own ***original*** Jolly Roger flag using the criteria and valued design features you established in Item 4 for an excellent flag. The smallest acceptable size is 9" × 12". The largest acceptable size is 18" × 24". *Use construction paper or cloth/material to make your flag.*

6. Your final project presentation should include the following:
   a. A written introduction/overview of the Jolly Roger flag's origin, history, and symbolism. Do this by incorporating the 25 note facts from Item 2.
   b. A neat display of the *five* different pirates and their flags. A paragraph about each pirate/flag should be next to each flag, capitalizing on the information you collected in Items 2 and 3.
   c. An original Jolly Roger flag that you created in Item 5.

Points: 20

	1	2	3	4
Effort/Personal Best	This work lacks effort. This needs work.	Your work shows moderate effort. You are capable of much more.	You did all that I asked you to. You could have stretched a bit more.	This is <u>your</u> best work! I don't think you could have done better. Awesome!
Presentation	Very messy. Quality is poor.	Parts are messy. Parts lack quality.	Neat. High quality.	Superbly done. Exemplary (I'd use this as a sample).
Completeness	Many parts are missing.	You are missing parts of the required tasks.	All tasks required are completed.	All tasks required are completed with extra details and/or additional work.
Accuracy and Quality of Thought	Information is incorrect or missing. Misinterpreted or lacks understanding of the subject.	Basic thinking. Some inaccuracies or misconceptions.	Critical thinking is beginning. Applies understanding of the subject matter.	Evidence of critical thinking. Sophisticated application of the subject.

SOURCE: Created by RJH teachers: K. Collyer, M. Coombs, M. Downer, J. Forrest, and J. Reese. Reprinted with permission from the Rye (NH) School Board.

Figure 8.10   Assess/Judge Task Card

Task Card—Assess/Judge (simple/evaluation): Film Review

1. Select a pirate film approved by a teacher and view.

    Check in with teacher. Teacher signature: _____

2. Take notes of the film based on
    a. characters,
    b. plot,
    c. setting, and
    d. themes.

    Check in with teacher. Teacher signature: _____

3. Write a five- to eight-sentence review that either recommends or does not recommend this film.

    Check in with teacher. Teacher signature: _____

4. The review should make reference to and include your opinion of
    a. the film overall,
    b. the portrayal of the main characters by lead players,
    c. the use of special effects, and
    d. the use of historical fact.

    Check in with teacher. Teacher signature: _____

5. The film should be cited as per page 7 in your agenda.

    Check in with teacher. Teacher signature: _____

Points: 10

	1	2	3	4
Effort/Personal Best	This work lacks effort. This needs work.	Your work shows moderate effort. You are capable of much more.	You did all that I asked you to. You could have stretched a bit more.	This is your best work! I don't think you could have done better. Awesome!
Presentation	Very messy. Quality is poor.	Parts are messy. Parts lack quality.	Neat. High quality.	Superbly done. Exemplary (I'd use this as a sample).
Completeness	Many parts are missing.	You are missing parts of the required tasks.	All tasks required are completed.	All tasks required are completed with extra details and/or additional work.
Accuracy and Quality of Thought	Information is incorrect or missing. Misinterpreted or lacks understanding of the subject.	Basic thinking. Some inaccuracies or misconceptions.	Critical thinking is beginning. Applies understanding of the subject matter.	Evidence of critical thinking. Sophisticated application of the subject.

SOURCE: Created by RJH teachers: K. Collyer, M. Coombs, M. Downer, J. Forrest, and J. Reese. Reprinted with permission from the Rye (NH) School Board.

Figure 8.11   Categorize Task Card

Task Card—Categorize (moderate/analysis): Diorama of Sea Life

1. Research using the IIM method and three resources the aquatic life native to the NH Seacoast and/or the Isles of Shoals.

   Check in with teacher. Teacher signature: _____

2. Write 20 note facts on marine life that you discovered.

   Check in with teacher. Teacher signature: _____

3. Using your note facts, sketch a design of a diorama (use 8.5″ × 11″ paper).

   Check in with teacher. Teacher signature: _____

4. Locate materials, assemble, and build diorama of NH sea life.

   Check in with teacher. Teacher signature: _____

Points: 20

	1	2	3	4
Effort/Personal Best	This work lacks effort. This needs work.	Your work shows moderate effort. You are capable of much more.	You did all that I asked you to. You could have stretched a bit more.	This is your best work! I don't think you could have done better. Awesome!
Presentation	Very messy. Quality is poor.	Parts are messy. Parts lack quality.	Neat. High quality.	Superbly done. Exemplary (I'd use this as a sample).
Completeness	Many parts are missing.	You are missing parts of the required tasks.	All tasks required are completed.	All tasks required are completed with extra details and/or additional work.
Accuracy and Quality of Thought	Information is incorrect or missing. Misinterpreted or lacks understanding of the subject.	Basic thinking. Some inaccuracies or misconceptions.	Critical thinking is beginning. Applies understanding of the subject matter.	Evidence of critical thinking. Sophisticated application of the subject.

SOURCE: Created by RJH teachers: K. Collyer, M. Coombs, M. Downer, J. Forrest, and J. Reese. Reprinted with permission from the Rye (NH) School Board.

Figure 8.12   Classify Task Card

Task Card—Classify/Identify (moderate/comprehension): Types of Privateer and Galleon Ships

1. Using the IIM method and three resources, research seafaring ships of the early pirates, privateers, and the shipping industry.

   Check in with teacher. Teacher signature:_____

2. Collect 20 note facts about the ships, their use, and their design.

   Check in with teacher. Teacher signature: _____

3. Using your note facts, design a set of "playing cards" for each of the types of ships you found along with specifications of the ships, such as size, types of sails, use of ships, number of masts, and positions of masts.

   Check in with teacher. Teacher signature: _____

4. For each of the ships, create a playing card with a picture/drawing of the ship on the front of the "card" and its specifications/important facts about the ship on the back.

   Check in with teacher. Teacher signature: _____

5. Using the playing cards, develop a card game in which the players must categorize the ships by different specifications. Be sure to include the rules of the game as a part of your final project.

   Check in with teacher. Teacher signature: _____

Points: 20

	1	2	3	4
Effort/Personal Best	This work lacks effort. This needs work.	Your work shows moderate effort. You are capable of much more.	You did all that I asked you to. You could have stretched a bit more.	This is your best work! I don't think you could have done better. Awesome!
Presentation	Very messy. Quality is poor.	Parts are messy. Parts lack quality.	Neat. High quality.	Superbly done. Exemplary (I'd use this as a sample).
Completeness	Many parts are missing.	You are missing parts of the required tasks.	All tasks required are completed.	All tasks required are completed with extra details and/or additional work.
Accuracy and Quality of Thought	Information is incorrect or missing. Misinterpreted or lacks understanding of the subject.	Basic thinking. Some inaccuracies or misconceptions.	Critical thinking is beginning. Applies understanding of the subject matter.	Evidence of critical thinking. Sophisticated application of the subject.

SOURCE: Created by RJH teachers: K. Collyer, M. Coombs, M. Downer, J. Forrest, and J. Reese. Reprinted with permission from the Rye (NH) School Board.

Figure 8.13   Compare Task Card

Task Card—Compare (simple/analysis): Two Cartoon Panels

1. Research and take notes of a fantasy pirate and a real pirate. (Use IIM and up to three resources plus 10 note facts on each pirate.)

    Check in with teacher. Teacher signature: _____

2. Make a list of four comparisons of both pirates.

ALIKE	DIFFERENT
_____	_____
_____	_____
_____	_____
_____	_____

    Check in with teacher. Teacher signature: _____

3. Use two 11″ × 8½″ pieces of paper (computer paper) to sketch each cartoon. Be sure to include all comparison ideas.

    Check in with teacher. Teacher signature: _____

4. On two pieces of 12″ × 18″ white drawing paper, create your cartoon drawings of each pirate. Be sure to label each pirate.

                                                                   Points: 10

	1	2	3	4
Effort/Personal Best	This work lacks effort. This needs work.	Your work shows moderate effort. You are capable of much more.	You did all that I asked you to. You could have stretched a bit more.	This is <u>your</u> best work! I don't think you could have done better. Awesome!
Presentation	Very messy. Quality is poor.	Parts are messy. Parts lack quality.	Neat. High quality.	Superbly done. Exemplary (I'd use this as a sample).
Completeness	Many parts are missing.	You are missing parts of the required tasks.	All tasks required are completed.	All tasks required are completed with extra details and/or additional work.
Accuracy and Quality of Thought	Information is incorrect or missing Misinterpreted or lacks understanding of the subject.	Basic thinking. Some inaccuracies or misconceptions.	Critical thinking is beginning. Applies understanding of the subject matter.	Evidence of critical thinking. Sophisticated application of the subject.

SOURCE: Created by RJH teachers: K. Collyer, M. Coombs, M. Downer, J. Forrest, and J. Reese. Reprinted with permission from the Rye (NH) School Board.

Figure 8.14   Construct Task Card

Task Card—Construct (moderate/application): Mobile of Isles of Shoals

1. Research the Isles of Shoals using IIM and three documented resources.

2. Collect at least 20 note facts.

   Check in with teacher. Teacher signature: _____

3. Create at least five components for your mobile. List them below using your note facts.

   a. _____

   b. _____

   c. _____

   d. _____

   e. _____

   Check in with teacher. Teacher signature: _____

4. Construct your mobile. Use your mobile rubric when you design it.

Points: 20

	1	2	3	4
Effort/Personal Best	This work lacks effort. This needs work.	Your work shows moderate effort. You are capable of much more.	You did all that I asked you to. You could have stretched a bit more.	This is <u>your</u> best work! I don't think you could have done better. Awesome!
Presentation	Very messy. Quality is poor.	Parts are messy. Parts lack quality.	Neat. High quality.	Superbly done. Exemplary (I'd use this as a sample).
Completeness	Many parts are missing.	You are missing parts of the required tasks.	All tasks required are completed.	All tasks required are completed with extra details and/or additional work.
Accuracy and Quality of Thought	Information is incorrect or missing. Misinterpreted or lacks understanding of the subject.	Basic thinking. Some inaccuracies or misconceptions.	Critical thinking is beginning. Applies understanding of the subject matter.	Evidence of critical thinking. Sophisticated application of the subject.

SOURCE: Created by RJH teachers: K. Collyer, M. Coombs, M. Downer, J. Forrest, and J. Reese. Reprinted with permission from the Rye (NH) School Board.

Figure 8.15   Create Task Card

Task Card—Create (moderate/synthesis):
Scrapbook of Female Pirates

1. Create a 10-page scrapbook.

2. Conduct research using IIM and three documented resources (one Web site only).

3. Collect at least 20 note facts (two per scrapbook page).

   Check in with teacher. Teacher signature: _____

4. The ten pages must include the following information:
   a. Birth (date and place) and death (date and place)
   b. Clothing typically worn
   c. Why became a pirate or privateer
   d. Famous pirate friends
   e. Main area of piracy (map)
   f. Ships typically sailed on, makeup of crew
   g. Work cited page
   h. Three subjects of your own choosing (fun/interesting facts or information)

   Check in with teacher. Teacher signature: _____

5. Include pictures (hand-drawn or traced) on each page with captions explaining information provided on that page.

6. Create a colorful and creative scrapbook cover with either hand-drawn or traced picture(s).

   Check in with teacher. Teacher signature: _____

Points: 20

	1	2	3	4
Effort/Personal Best	This work lacks effort. This needs work.	Your work shows moderate effort. You are capable of much more.	You did all that I asked you to. You could have stretched a bit more.	This is your best work! I don't think you could have done better. Awesome!
Presentation	Very messy. Quality is poor.	Parts are messy. Parts lack quality.	Neat. High quality.	Superbly done. Exemplary (I'd use this as a sample).
Completeness	Many parts are missing.	You are missing parts of the required tasks.	All tasks required are completed.	All tasks required are completed with extra details and/or additional work.
Accuracy and Quality of Thought	Information is incorrect or missing. Misinterpreted or lacks understanding of the subject.	Basic thinking. Some inaccuracies or misconceptions.	Critical thinking is beginning. Applies understanding of the subject matter.	Evidence of critical thinking. Sophisticated application of the subject.

SOURCE: Created by RJH teachers: K. Collyer, M. Coombs, M. Downer, J. Forrest, and J. Reese. Reprinted with permission from the Rye (NH) School Board.

Figure 8.16   Draw Task Card

Task Card—Draw (simple/synthesis): Chart the Course

1. Locate a chart of the world (use this Web site: http://www.nationalgeographic.com/expeditions/atlas/) and expand to an 11″ × 17″ size. Mount on oak tag or construction paper.

   Check in with teacher. Teacher signature: _____

2. Research an actual pirate shipwreck using IIM and up to three resources including the following Web sites:
   a. National Geographic: Pirate Ship Whydah (http://www.nationalgeographic.com/explorer/whydah/more.html)
   b. National Geographic: Pirates of the Whydah (http://www.nationalgeographic.com/whydah/story.html)
   c. Pirates and Privateers
   d. Queen Anne's Revenge
   e. Treasure Hunt: Aye, There Be Pirates Here
   f. http://www.melfisher.org/shipwrecks.htm

   Check in with teacher. Teacher signature: _____

3. Collect at least 15 note facts answering the following questions:
   a. What type of ship was it?
   b. Who were the captain and crew?
   c. What was the cargo/treasure it carried?
   d. What was its destination?
   e. Has it been salvaged? By whom and when?

   Check in with teacher. Teacher signature: _____

4. On the chart, plot and track a course from Rye, New Hampshire, to the location of the wreck and sunken treasure.

   Check in with teacher. Teacher signature: _____

5. On the chart, plot and track the captain's course that led up to the wreck.

   Check in with teacher. Teacher signature: _____

6. Prepare key and clearly written labels for your finished chart.

Points: 10

SOURCE: Created by RJH teachers: K. Collyer, M. Coombs, M. Downer, J. Forrest, and J. Reese. Reprinted with permission from the Rye (NH) School Board.

Figure 8.17   Evaluate Task Card

Task Card—Evaluate (complex/synthesis):
PowerPoint Presentation

1. Design a PowerPoint presentation with 10 slides. Create a title for your presentation.

2. Conduct research using IIM and three resources. Collect at least 30 note facts.

   Check in with teacher. Teacher signature: _____

3. Collect at least 10 images of pirates portrayed in a variety of media formats (movies, cartoons, TV shows, newspapers, magazines, books).

   Check in with teacher. Teacher signature: _____

4. Include three sound effects or a song.

   Check in with teacher. Teacher signature: _____

5. Three slides will include images and text that give examples of how pirates are portrayed.

   Check in with teacher. Teacher signature: _____

6. Three slides will include images and text explaining about actual pirates from history and present day.

   Check in with teacher. Teacher signature: _____

7. Two slides should address the ideas of the stereotypes (both positive and negative) of pirate life.

   Check in with teacher. Teacher signature: _____

8. One slide will include the works cited information (see page 7 in your agenda).

   Check in with teacher. Teacher signature: _____

Points: 30

	1	**2**	**3**	**4**
Effort/Personal Best	This work lacks effort. This needs work.	Your work shows moderate effort. You are capable of much more.	You did all that I asked you to. You could have stretched a bit more.	This is <u>your</u> best work! I don't think you could have done better. Awesome!
Presentation	Very messy. Quality is poor.	Parts are messy. Parts lack quality.	Neat. High quality.	Superbly done. Exemplary (I'd use this as a sample).
Completeness	Many parts are missing.	You are missing parts of the required tasks.	All tasks required are completed.	All tasks required are completed with extra details and/or additional work.
Accuracy and Quality of Thought	Information is incorrect or missing. Misinterpreted or lacks understanding of the subject.	Basic thinking. Some inaccuracies or misconceptions.	Critical thinking is beginning. Applies understanding of the subject matter.	Evidence of critical thinking. Sophisticated application of the subject.

SOURCE: Created by RJH teachers: K. Collyer, M. Coombs, M. Downer, J. Forrest, and J. Reese. Reprinted with permission from the Rye (NH) School Board.

Figure 8.18   Identify Task Card

Task Card—Identify (simple/knowledge): Poster of Natural Resources

1. Research, using IIM and up to three resources, the natural resources required for building and sailing (including the ships themselves, sails, and ropes). Collect up to 20 note facts.

    Check in with teacher. Teacher signature: _____

2. Create a poster on 11″ × 17″ paper that identifies at least three of these products that are derived from a natural resource (see Item 1).

    Check in with teacher. Teacher signature: _____

3. Create three images either by tracing or freehand drawing.

    Check in with teacher. Teacher signature: _____

4. The poster should also answer the following questions:
    a. What are the resources that ship materials are made of?
    b. Where in the world were these resources harvested or mined?
    c. How much or how many of these resources were required to run a ship? (Be specific about ship name and size for your example.)
    d. What are the resources that ship materials are made of?
    e. Where in the world were these resources harvested or mined?
    f. How much or how many of these resources were required to run a ship? (Be specific about ship name and size for your example.)

    Check in with teacher. Teacher signature: _____

5. The poster should be visual with good use of color, balance, and images.

6. The poster should be professional looking. (Neat, showing care in lettering and spelling, and in its final form.)

Points: 10

	1	2	3	4
Effort/Personal Best	This work lacks effort.	Your work shows moderate effort.	You did all that I asked you to.	This is <u>your</u> best work!
	This needs work.	You are capable of much more.	You could have stretched a bit more.	I don't think you could have done better. Awesome!
Presentation	Very messy.	Parts are messy.	Neat.	Superbly done.
	Quality is poor.	Parts lack quality.	High quality.	Exemplary (I'd use this as a sample).
Completeness	Many parts are missing.	You are missing parts of the required tasks.	All tasks required are completed.	All tasks required are completed with extra details and/or additional work.
Accuracy and Quality of Thought	Information is incorrect or missing.	Basic thinking.	Critical thinking is beginning.	Evidence of critical thinking.
	Misinterpreted or lacks understanding of the subject.	Some inaccuracies or misconceptions.	Applies understanding of the subject matter.	Sophisticated application of the subject.

SOURCE: Created by RJH teachers: K. Collyer, M. Coombs, M. Downer, J. Forrest, and J. Reese. Reprinted with permission from the Rye (NH) School Board.

Figure 8.19   Illustrate Task Card

***Task Card*—Illustrate (simple/application): Illustrate Your
Favorite Part of *The Black Pirate***

1. Choose your favorite part of *The Black Pirate*. Think about how you could draw a picture of that story part.

2. Make a list of five objects or people that you would include in your drawing.

    a. _____

    b. _____

    c. _____

    d. _____

    e. _____

    Check in with teacher. Teacher signature: _____

3. On an 11″ × 8½″ piece of paper (computer paper), sketch your drawing with all five points included.

    Check in with teacher. Teacher signature: _____

4. On a 12″ × 18″ sheet of white paper, draw your colorful picture.

                                   Points: 20

	1	2	3	4
Effort/Personal Best	This work lacks effort. This needs work.	Your work shows moderate effort. You are capable of much more.	You did all that I asked you to. You could have stretched a bit more.	This is <u>your</u> best work! I don't think you could have done better. Awesome!
Presentation	Very messy. Quality is poor.	Parts are messy. Parts lack quality.	Neat. High quality.	Superbly done. Exemplary (I'd use this as a sample).
Completeness	Many parts are missing.	You are missing parts of the required tasks.	All tasks required are completed.	All tasks required are completed with extra details and/or additional work.
Accuracy and Quality of Thought	Information is incorrect or missing. Misinterpreted or lacks understanding of the subject.	Basic thinking. Some inaccuracies or misconceptions.	Critical thinking is beginning. Applies understanding of the subject matter.	Evidence of critical thinking. Sophisticated application of the subject.

SOURCE: Created by RJH teachers: K. Collyer, M. Coombs, M. Downer, J. Forrest, and J. Reese. Reprinted with permission from the Rye (NH) School Board.

Figure 8.20   List/Order Task Card

Task Card—List/Order (moderate/knowledge): Time Line

1. Research pirates using IIM and three documented resources (no more than one Web site).

   Check in with teacher. Teacher signature: _____

2. Collect 20 note facts.

   Check in with teacher. Teacher signature: _____

3. Create a time line of pirate history for a given time period, size 11" × 17". Include at least 20 significant events. This includes date and description of who was involved.

   Check in with teacher. Teacher signature: _____

4. Include at least five original drawings (hand-drawn or traced) that go along with your date and description.

   Check in with teacher. Teacher signature: _____

5. Write final copy. Make sure it is neat, writing is clear, color is used, sequencing is correct, and spelling is correct. Use only one side of your paper. Cite your references. (Include this on the back of your time line.)

Points: 20

	1	2	3	4
Effort/Personal Best	This work lacks effort. This needs work.	Your work shows moderate effort. You are capable of much more.	You did all that I asked you to. You could have stretched a bit more.	This is <u>your</u> best work! I don't think you could have done better. Awesome!
Presentation	Very messy. Quality is poor.	Parts are messy. Parts lack quality.	Neat. High quality.	Superbly done. Exemplary (I'd use this as a sample).
Completeness	Many parts are missing.	You are missing parts of the required tasks.	All tasks required are completed.	All tasks required are completed with extra details and/or additional work.
Accuracy and Quality of Thought	Information is incorrect or missing. Misinterpreted or lacks understanding of the subject.	Basic thinking. Some inaccuracies or misconceptions.	Critical thinking is beginning. Applies understanding of the subject matter.	Evidence of critical thinking. Sophisticated application of the subject.

SOURCE: Created by RJH teachers: K. Collyer, M. Coombs, M. Downer, J. Forrest, and J. Reese. Reprinted with permission from the Rye (NH) School Board.

Figure 8.21   Memorize Task Card

Task Card—Memorize (complex/knowledge): Oral Interpretation

1. Read a pirate-related novel from the list.

   Check in with teacher. Teacher signature: _____

2. Choose one or two passages from the novel to memorize and interpret.

   Check in with teacher. Teacher signature: _____

3. Prepare a presentation that will be done in character or as a narrator that includes the following:
   a. Recitation of the selected passage.
   b. The interpretation of the passage with reference to character, plot, and theme.
   c. A brief introduction that sets up the selection.
   d. Presentation is no more that five minutes and no shorter than three.

   Check in with teacher. Teacher signature: _____

4. Record your presentation on video.

Points: 30

	1	2	3	4
Effort/Personal Best	This work lacks effort. This needs work.	Your work shows moderate effort. You are capable of much more.	You did all that I asked you to. You could have stretched a bit more.	This is your best work! I don't think you could have done better. Awesome!
Presentation	Very messy. Quality is poor.	Parts are messy. Parts lack quality.	Neat. High quality.	Superbly done. Exemplary (I'd use this as a sample).
Completeness	Many parts are missing.	You are missing parts of the required tasks.	All tasks required are completed.	All tasks required are completed with extra details and/or additional work.
Accuracy and Quality of Thought	Information is incorrect or missing. Misinterpreted or lacks understanding of the subject.	Basic thinking. Some inaccuracies or misconceptions.	Critical thinking is beginning. Applies understanding of the subject matter.	Evidence of critical thinking. Sophisticated application of the subject.

SOURCE: Created by RJH teachers: K. Collyer, M. Coombs, M. Downer, J. Forrest, and J. Reese. Reprinted with permission from the Rye (NH) School Board.

Figure 8.22 Produce Task Card

Task Card—Produce (complex/synthesis): Nine-Panel Comic Strip

1. Research either *privateers* or *buccaneers* using IIM and up to three resources.

   Check in with teacher. Teacher signature: _____

2. Collect up to 30 note facts about your topic.

   Check in with teacher. Teacher signature: _____

3. Create a character that typifies your topic and, using text and drawings, create a nine-panel comic book on an 11″ × 17″ piece of paper.

   Check in with teacher. Teacher signature: _____

4. Your comic strip should do the following:
   a. Clearly define the topic.
   b. Show how your topic differs from pirates/privateers/buccaneers.
   c. Discuss the lifestyle, rewards, and risks of their occupation.
   d. Tell a story.

   Check in with teacher. Teacher signature: _____

5. Cite your sources properly using your agenda on page 7.

   Check in with teacher. Teacher signature: _____

Points: 30

	1	2	3	4
Effort/Personal Best	This work lacks effort. This needs work.	Your work shows moderate effort. You are capable of much more.	You did all that I asked you to. You could have stretched a bit more.	This is <u>your</u> best work! I don't think you could have done better. Awesome!
Presentation	Very messy. Quality is poor.	Parts are messy. Parts lack quality.	Neat. High quality.	Superbly done. Exemplary (I'd use this as a sample).
Completeness	Many parts are missing.	You are missing parts of the required tasks.	All tasks required are completed.	All tasks required are completed with extra details and/or additional work.
Accuracy and Quality of Thought	Information is incorrect or missing. Misinterpreted or lacks understanding of the subject.	Basic thinking. Some inaccuracies or misconceptions.	Critical thinking is beginning. Applies understanding of the subject matter.	Evidence of critical thinking. Sophisticated application of the subject.

SOURCE: Created by RJH teachers: K. Collyer, M. Coombs, M. Downer, J. Forrest, and J. Reese. Reprinted with permission from the Rye (NH) School Board.

Figure 8.23 Research Task Card

Task Card—Research (simple/knowledge):
Share After Reading a Nonfiction Novel About Pirates

1. Using IIM and one documented print resource, select a specific research topic related to pirates.

   Check in with teacher. Teacher's signature: _____

2. Write three essential questions about the topic.

   Check in with teacher. Teacher's signature: _____

3. Write 15–20 note facts that answer the essential questions.

   Check in with teacher. Teacher's signature: _____

4. Organize your note facts and write an essay with a paragraph on each essential question.

   Check in with teacher. Teacher's signature: _____

Points: 10

	1	2	3	4
Effort/Personal Best	This work lacks effort. This needs work.	Your work shows moderate effort. You are capable of much more.	You did all that I asked you to. You could have stretched a bit more.	This is your best work! I don't think you could have done better. Awesome!
Presentation	Very messy. Quality is poor.	Parts are messy. Parts lack quality.	Neat. High quality.	Superbly done. Exemplary (I'd use this as a sample).
Completeness	Many parts are missing.	You are missing parts of the required tasks.	All tasks required are completed.	All tasks required are completed with extra details and/or additional work.
Accuracy and Quality of Thought	Information is incorrect or missing. Misinterpreted or lacks understanding of the subject.	Basic thinking. Some inaccuracies or misconceptions.	Critical thinking is beginning. Applies understanding of the subject matter.	Evidence of critical thinking. Sophisticated application of the subject.

SOURCE: Created by RJH teachers: K. Collyer, M. Coombs, M. Downer, J. Forrest, and J. Reese. Reprinted with permission from the Rye (NH) School Board.

Figure 8.24   Select Task Card

Task Card—Select (complex/comprehension): Pirate ABC Book

1. Read a novel such as *The Buccaneers* or another novel from the RJH list.

2. Keep a list of vocabulary from A–Z and/or characters starting with the letters of the alphabet. Write a sentence about each word from A–Z as it relates to your novel. Have one vocabulary word, one sentence, and one picture for each letter of the alphabet.

   Check in with teacher. Teacher signature: _____

3. Type each letter and the describing sentence on 26 pages of 11" × 8½" paper.

   Check in with teacher. Teacher signature: _____

4. Draw a colorful picture for each letter on each page. Be creative.

5. Design a cover for your Pictionary book.

Points: 30

	1	2	3	4
Effort/Personal Best	This work lacks effort. This needs work.	Your work shows moderate effort. You are capable of much more.	You did all that I asked you to. You could have stretched a bit more.	This is <u>your</u> best work! I don't think you could have done better. Awesome!
Presentation	Very messy. Quality is poor.	Parts are messy. Parts lack quality.	Neat. High quality.	Superbly done. Exemplary (I'd use this as a sample).
Completeness	Many parts are missing.	You are missing parts of the required tasks.	All tasks required are completed.	All tasks required are completed with extra details and/or additional work.
Accuracy and Quality of Thought	Information is incorrect or missing. Misinterpreted or lacks understanding of the subject.	Basic thinking. Some inaccuracies or misconceptions.	Critical thinking is beginning. Applies understanding of the subject matter.	Evidence of critical thinking. Sophisticated application of the subject.

SOURCE: Created by RJH teachers: K. Collyer, M. Coombs, M. Downer, J. Forrest, and J. Reese. Reprinted with permission from the Rye (NH) School Board.

Figure 8.25 Teach Task Card

Task Card—Teach (complex/application): Music of the Sea

1. Research using IIM and three resources pirate songs or songs of the sea. Many songs you may find will not be appropriate for school, so you may want to ask teachers in this grade for ideas of where to find them or for copies of songs.

   Check in with teacher. Teacher signature: _____

2. Collect at least 30 note facts answering the following questions:
   a. What is a sea shanty?
   b. What are the different types of sea shanties?
   c. What are examples of the different categories of shanties?

   Check in with teacher. Teacher signature: _____

3. Using the "midi" and a musical composition software program, compose a sea-related song with lyrics and melody. The song must include at least one chorus and one verse.

   Check in with teacher. Teacher signature: _____

4. Record a performance of your original song as the final project.

   Check in with teacher. Teacher signature: _____

Points: 30

	1	2	3	4
Effort/Personal Best	This work lacks effort. This needs work.	Your work shows moderate effort. You are capable of much more.	You did all that I asked you to. You could have stretched a bit more.	This is your best work! I don't think you could have done better. Awesome!
Presentation	Very messy. Quality is poor.	Parts are messy. Parts lack quality.	Neat. High quality.	Superbly done. Exemplary (I'd use this as a sample).
Completeness	Many parts are missing.	You are missing parts of the required tasks.	All tasks required are completed.	All tasks required are completed with extra details and/or additional work.
Accuracy and Quality of Thought	Information is incorrect or missing. Misinterpreted or lacks understanding of the subject.	Basic thinking. Some inaccuracies or misconceptions.	Critical thinking is beginning. Applies understanding of the subject matter.	Evidence of critical thinking. Sophisticated application of the subject.

SOURCE: Created by RJH teachers: K. Collyer, M. Coombs, M. Downer, J. Forrest, and J. Reese. Reprinted with permission from the Rye (NH) School Board.

Figure 8.26   Pirate Reality Check!

Name _____   Circle one: ASA   EAF   NAS

Response Questions: Select one question to answer. Write in paragraph form with a topic sentence and details (TS + 4) and a closing sentence. Proofread your writing before turning it in, making sure it says what you want it to say.

1. What are the common stereotypes used in the Disney films that were discussed in class? (We discussed *The Lion King, Snow White, Cinderella, Sleeping Beauty, Little Mermaid,* and *Peter Pan.*) Give examples.

2. What are the messages being sent to viewers about any given stereotypes in these films? (Especially if they watch one over and over and over and over again.)

3. Explain the typical formula for any of the films that we have viewed in school for the pirate unit. Give examples of characters, setting, themes, and plot. (We have seen *Captain Blood, The Seahawk, The Black Pirate,* and *Pirates of the Caribbean.*)

4. Compare and contrast (alike or not like one another) pirates and their activities to terrorists of today. Create a Venn diagram to organize your thoughts.

5. Recommend a film that you have seen that does not follow the typical Hollywood formula. Give examples of how it is different (and be sure to give film details such as title, stars, etc.)

6. Many of the antagonists in the Disney films have physical problems (scars, disabilities, speech impediments) or they are shown to be unattractive in some way (fat, big noses, warts, etc.). How can Hollywood fix the idea that "ugly people" are evil? Come up with examples to support your ideas.

7. How do stereotypes and prejudices affect how you think about or deal with people in your own life?

Use the appropriate words or expressions below in your responses:

stereotype	images	realistic	unrealistic
prejudice	race	occupation	gender
appearances	character	antagonist	protagonist
negative	positive	fear	target
media	ethnic	religious	perceptions
labels	judgments	villain	hero/heroine
comic relief	sidekicks	influence	

SOURCE: Created by RJH teachers: K. Collyer, M. Coombs, M. Downer, J. Forrest, and J. Reese. Reprinted with permission from the Rye (NH) School Board.

Glossary

Adequate Yearly Progress (AYP). A measure of the federal government's accountability system for schools under No Child Left Behind. It is a combination of student performance, student participation, and school progress over time. Schools that do not demonstrate AYP for two consecutive years are identified as needing improvement and subject to immediate interventions—beginning with technical assistance and then more serious corrective actions if the school continues to not make AYP.

Assessment. An evaluation of student, teacher, and school performance.

Bloom's Taxonomy. A classification by Dr. Benjamin Bloom that organized six levels of thinking based on a hierarchal order: knowledge, comprehension, application, analysis, synthesis, and evaluation.

Components of Professional Practice. The components of professional practice are a part of a comprehensive framework reflecting the many different aspects of teaching, as developed by Charlotte Danielson.

Curriculum Mapping. A teacher-driven, dynamic process that documents the real and expected curriculum experiences of a student.

Curriculum Standards. Written statements, by national, state, or local education authorities, of what is to be taught.

Differentiated Instruction. Instruction that is geared to diverse learners in a classroom and offers activities that vary in content, process, and product.

Content	Topic to be learned
Process	Means by which students use key skills to understand the content
Product	Evidence of what students have learned and the basis for further learning

Direct Instruction. A system of teaching in which teachers deliver clear instructions and assist students in generalizing information and skills.

Domain. A broad category of teaching responsibilities under Charlotte Danielson's *Enhancing Professional Practice: A Framework for Teaching.*

Essential Questions. Unit questions that raise big ideas, hook the student's interest, and are generally aimed at higher order thinking skills.

Gardner's Multiple Intelligences. A schema developed by Howard Gardner that identified eight distinct intelligences and suggested that each person has a lead intelligence.

Bodily-Kinesthetic Intelligence	Person possessing this intelligence has the ability to control body movement and learns through use of both gross and fine motor skills
Interpersonal Intelligence	Person possessing this intelligence has the ability to relate to others and learns through working collaboratively
Intrapersonal Intelligence	Person possessing this intelligence has the ability to self-reflect and learns through working alone
Logical-Mathematical Intelligence	Person possessing this intelligence has the ability to use reason, logic, and numbers and learns through making pattern connections and computation
Musical Intelligence	Person possessing this intelligence has the ability to produce and appreciate music and learns through sounds and rhythms
Naturalist Intelligence	Person possessing this intelligence has the ability to categorize things and observe nature and learns though collecting and studying a group of objects
Verbal-Linguistic Intelligence	Person possessing this intelligence has the ability to use words and language and learns through reading, writing, and speaking
Visual-Spatial Intelligence	Person possessing this intelligence has the ability to perceive visually and learns through pictures and image manipulation

Goals 2000: Educate America Act. A federal law, enacted in 1994, that required by the year 2000 that all students leaving Grades 4, 8, and 12 will demonstrate competency over challenging subject matter including English, mathematics, science, foreign languages, civics and government, economics, art, history, and geography.

Individuals With Disabilities Education Improvement Act. The reauthorization of the Individuals With Disabilities Education Act (IDEA) that emphasizes requirements for special education teachers to be highly qualified, using up to 15 percent of entitlement funds to help struggling students before they are referred to special education, and requirements to consider a student's response to scientifically based programs as a factor in determining if the student has a learning disability.

Interdisciplinary Units. An approach that thoughtfully incorporates and connects key concepts and skills from many disciplines into the presentation of a single unit.

Learning Styles. A method of classifying learners according to their preference for a particular way of thinking.

Sensing-Thinking Learners	Organized, efficient, active learners who focus more on ideas than people
Intuitive-Thinking Learners	Logical probers who want to understand complex problems
Intuitive-Feeling Learners	Highly imaginative, unconventional students who prefer to follow their own path to learning
Sensing-Feeling Learners	Emotionally involved students who are interested in learning about situations concerning living things rather than cold hard facts

Mastery Learning. An instructional model developed by John Carroll and Benjamin Bloom that emphasizes using multiple strategies to achieve student mastery of a topic before beginning another topic.

Mastery Teaching. A plan for teaching developed by Madeline Hunter that includes knowing the objectives for the lesson, the prerequisite skills, and the performance standards. She also suggested the use of an anticipatory hook to motivate students and Bloom's taxonomy to extend their thinking.

Metacognition. Thinking about thinking; the ability to know what we know and do not know.

A Nation at Risk: The Imperative for Educational Reform. A 1983 study, prepared by the U.S. Secretary of Education and others, that illustrated

- lack of consistency among curricula,
- lack of emphasis on higher order thinking skills, and
- pervasive mediocrity among teachers.

Neurons. Cells of the brain.

No Child Left Behind Act. Bipartisan legislation, which mandated

- new requirements for highly qualified teachers,
- the use of scientifically based research,
- stronger assessment requirements, and
- strict accountability rules for school districts.

Performance Standards. Articulated expectations for what students must be able to demonstrate after instruction in the required content.

Responsive Classroom. A program for developing respect and rapport within the classroom.

Rubrics. Scoring tools that specifically state the criteria for and a performance scale regarding the salient aspects of a long-term project.

Skill. Ability to complete a task; dexterity.

Standards Movement. A movement of professionals and parents that wants state and local curriculum frameworks developed in order to standardize the content and assessment of what students are learning.

Understanding by Design. A model of lesson planning that suggests teachers must know the intended outcome of the lesson first and then design the lesson backward to achieve that outcome.

References

Armstrong, T. (2000). *Multiple intelligences in the classroom.* Alexandria, VA: ASCD.

Arter, J., & McTighe, J. (2001). *Scoring rubrics in the classroom: Using performance criteria for assessing and improving student performance* (p. 8). Thousand Oaks, CA: Corwin Press.

Bloom, B. (1956). *Taxonomy of educational objectives: The classification of educational goals, handbook 1. Cognitive domain.* New York: Longmans, Green.

Bloom, B. (1971). Master learning. In J. H. Block (Ed.), *Mastery learning: Theory and practice.* New York: Holt, Rinehart & Winston.

Carroll, J. (1971). Problems of measurement related to the concept of learning for mastery. In J. H. Block (Ed.), *Mastery learning: Theory and practice.* New York: Holt, Rinehart & Winston.

Clithero, C. (2004). *Bridges unit.* Rye, NH: Rye School District.

Cooper, H. (2001). *The battle over homework* (2nd ed., pp. 14–63). Thousand Oaks, CA: Corwin Press.

Costa, A., & Kallick, B. (2004). *Assessment strategies for self-directed learning* (p. 27). Thousand Oaks, CA: Corwin Press.

Danielson, C. (1996). *Enhancing professional practice: A framework for teaching* (pp. 65–90). Alexandria, VA: ASCD.

Erickson, H. L. (2002). *Concept-based curriculum and instruction: Teaching beyond the facts* (p. 51). Thousand Oaks, CA: Corwin Press.

Gardner, H. (1983). *Frames of mind: The theory of multiple intelligences tenth anniversary edition.* New York: Basic Books.

Gardner, H. (1999). *Intelligence reframed: Multiple intelligences for the 21st century.* New York: Basic Books.

Gentile, J. R., & Lalley, J. (2003). *Standards and mastery learning* (pp. 95–96). Thousand Oaks, CA: Corwin Press.

Gladwell, M. (2002). *The tipping point: How little things can make a big difference* (pp. 7–9). Boston, MA: Back Bay Books, Little, Brown and Company.

H.R. 1804, Goals 2000: Educate America Act, Section 102 (3), (1994).

Hoyle, J. R., English, F. W., & Steffy, B. E. (1990). *Skills for successful school leaders* (2nd ed., p. 98). Arlington, VA: AASA.

Hunter, R. (2004). *Madeline Hunter's mastery teaching: Increasing instructional effectiveness in elementary and secondary schools* (Updated ed.). Thousand Oaks, CA: Corwin Press.

Individuals With Disabilities Education Improvement Act, Pub. L. 108-446 (2004).

Jacobs, H. (1997) *Mapping the big picture* (pp. 5, 61). Alexandria, VA: ASCD.

Jacobs, H. (2005). *Mapping active literacy.* Paper presented at the conference of the Curriculum Mapping Institute, Snowbird, UT.

Jukes, I. (2005). *Moving the educational debate.* Retrieved March 2005 from http://www.thecommittedsardine.net/infosavvy/education/handouts/handouts.asp?mid=1

Kallick, B. (2005). *Mapping as a hub.* Paper presented at the conference of the Curriculum Mapping Institute, Snowbird, UT.

Kenney, C. (2005, January 10). Teacher suspended over grading [Electronic version]. *Louisville Kentucky Courier Journal*. Retrieved January 2005 from http:\\wwwcourier-journal.com/localnews/2005/01/05ky/B1-male0105-6043.html

Kid Source.com. *How important is homework?* Retrieved May 11, 2005, from http:\\www.kidsource.com/kidsource/content/HOW_IMPORTANT_HOMEWORK.HTML

Kriete, R. (2002). *The morning meeting book*. Greenfield, MA: Northeast Foundation for Children.

Marzano, R., Pickering, D., & Pollock, J. (2001). *Classroom instruction that works*. Alexandria, VA: ASCD.

Marzano, R. (2003). *What works in schools: Translating research in action* (pp. 140–141). Alexandria, VA: ASCD.

McTighe, J. (1997). What happens between assessments? *Educational Leadership, 54*(4), 6.

National Commission on Excellence in Education. (1983). *A nation at risk: The imperative for educational reform*. Washington, DC: U.S. Government Printing Office.

New Hampshire Department of Education. (1993a). *New Hampshire state frameworks for social studies standards and proficiencies*. Concord, NH: Author.

New Hampshire Department of Education (1993b). *New Hampshire state frameworks for mathematics*. Concord, NH: Author.

No Child Left Behind Act of 2001, Pub. L. No. 107-110 (2002).

O'Shea, M. (2005). *From standards to success* (pp. 64–65). Alexandria, VA: ASCD.

Plymouth State University. (1995). *New Hampshire state frameworks for science, NH K–6 science curriculum addendum*. Plymouth, NH: Author.

Quaglia, R. (2004). *"My Voice" survey provides meaningful school profiles*. Beverly, MA: Global Institute for Student Aspirations.

Rye Junior High School Teachers. (2002). *Pirates unit*. Rye, NH: Rye School District.

School Administrative Unit 50. (2004). *Science curriculum: Student proficiencies*. Greenland, NH: Author.

Stiggins, R. (2005) *Assessment for learning: Creating a culture of confidence*. Paper presented at the conference of the Curriculum Mapping Institute, Snowbird, UT.

Strong, R. W., Silver, H., & Perini, M. (2000). *So each may learn: Integrating learning styles and multiple intelligences*. Alexandria, VA: ASCD.

Strong, R. W., Silver, H., & Perini, M. (2001). *Teaching what matters most* (p. 1). Alexandria, VA: ASCD.

Stronge, J. (2002). *Qualities of effective teachers* (pp. 14–19). Alexandria, VA: ASCD.

Tomlinson, C. (1999). *The differentiated classroom: Responding to the needs of all learners* (p. 11). Alexandria, VA: ASCD.

Tomlinson, C. (2000, September). Reconcilable differences? Standards based teaching and differentiation. *Educational Leadership, 58*(1) 6–11.

Tomlinson, C. (2001). *How to differentiate instruction in mixed ability classrooms* (p. 74). Alexandria, VA: ASCD.

Wiggins, G., & McTighe, J. (1998). *Understanding by design*. Alexandria, VA: ASCD.

Wolfe, P. (2001). *Brain matters: Translating research into classroom practice* (p. 99). Alexandria, VA: ASCD.

Zull, J. (2002). *The art of changing the brain: Enriching the practice of teaching by exploring the biology of learning* (p. 93). Sterling, VA: Stylus.

Additional Resources

Adkins, J. (2002). *Bridges: From my side to yours.* Brookfield, CT: Roaring Books Press.

Ashman, H. (Producer). (1989). *The little mermaid* [Motion picture]. United States: Buena Vista.

Avi. (1977). *Captain Grey.* New York: Pantheon Books.

Brett, J. (1991). *Berlioz the bear.* New York: Putnam.

Bruckheimer, J. (Producer). (2003). *Pirates of the Caribbean: The curse of the black pearl* [Motion picture]. United States: Buena Vista.

Burns, K. (Director). (1982). *Brooklyn bridge* [Documentary]. (Available from PBS Home Video)

Carter, P. (1992). *The bridge book.* New York: Simon & Schuster.

Curtiz, M. (Director). (1935). *Captain Blood* [Motion picture]. United States: Warner Brothers.

Curtiz, M. (Director). (1940). *The sea hawk* [Motion picture]. United States: Warner Brothers.

Disney, W. (Producer). (1937). *Snow White* [Motion picture]. United States: RKO Radio Pictures.

Disney, W. (Producer). (1950). *Cinderella* [Motion picture]. United States: RKO Radio Pictures.

Disney, W. (Producer). (1953). *Peter Pan* [Motion picture]. United States: RKO Radio Pictures.

Disney, W. (Producer). (1959). *Sleeping beauty* [Motion picture]. United States: Buena Vista.

DiSalvo-Ryan, D. (1993). *City green.* New York: Morrow Junior Books.

Dispezio, M. (2002). *Map mania: Discovering where you are and getting to where you aren't.* New York: Sterling Publishing.

Doyle, B. (1990). *Covered bridge.* Toronto: Groundwood/Douglas & McIntyre.

Editors of *Time for Kids* (Ed.) & Satterfield, K. H. (2005). *Benjamin Franklin: A man of many talents.* New York: HarperCollins.

Ehlert, L. (1991). *Red leaf, yellow leaf.* San Diego: Harcourt Brace Jovanovich.

Erdich, L. (2002). *Bears make rock soup.* San Francisco: Children's Book Press.

Galdone, P. (1981). *The three billy goats gruff.* New York: Clarion.

Gillooly, J. (1926). *The black pirate* [Motion picture]. United States: United Artists.

Hahn, D. (Producer), Allers, R., & Minkoff, R. (Directors). (1994). *The lion king* [Motion picture]. United States: Disney.

Harper, C. M. (2001). *Imaginative inventions: The who, what, where, when, and why of roller skates, potato chips, marbles, and pie and more!* Boston: Little, Brown.

Hirschi, R. (1991). *Summer.* New York: Cobblehill Books.

Johmann, C. (1999). *Bridges: Amazing structures to design, build, and test.* Charlotte, VT: Williamson.

Kalman, B. (1999). *What is a community from A to Z?* New York: Crabtree Publishing.

Kaner, E. (1995). *Bridges.* Toronto: Kids Can Press.

Lawrence, I. (2001). *The buccaneers.* New York: Delacorte Press.

Leslie, C. W. (1991). *Nature all year long.* New York: Greenwillow Books.

Macauley, D. (Host). (2000). Building big: Bridges [Television series episode]. In L. Klein (Producer), *Building big.* Boston: WGBH.

Mann, E., & Witschonke, A. (1996). *The Brooklyn Bridge: A wonders of the world book.* New York: Mikaya Press.

Marrin, A. (1999). *Terror of the Spanish Main: Sir Henry Morgan and his buccaneers.* New York: Dutton Children's Books.

Marsh, C. (2003). *The mystery of Blackbeard the pirate* (Carole Marsh Mysteries Series). Peachtree City, GA: Gallopade Intl.

Ortabasi, O. (Director). *On the wings of the monarch* [Motion picture]. United States: The Dreaming Tree.

Paterson, K. (1987). *Bridge to Terabithia.* New York: Harper Trophy Books.

Penn, A. (2004). *Mystery at Blackbeard's cove.* Terre Haute, IN: Tanglewood Press.

Petroski, H. (1995). *Engineers of dreams: Great bridge builders and the spanning of America.* New York: Knopf.

Provensen, A., & Provensen, M. (2001). New York: Aladdin Paperbacks.

Rees, C. (2003). *Pirates!: The true and remarkable adventures of Minerva Sharpe and Nancy Kington, female pirates.* New York: Bloomsbury.

Scieszka, J. (2002). *Hey kid, want to buy a bridge?* New York: Viking Press.

Seiler, B. (1997). How the West Was Negative One [Computer software]. New York: Sunburst Technology.

Silver, J., & Donner, R. (1987). *Lethal weapon* [Motion picture]. United States: Warner Brothers.

Simon, P., & Garfunkel, A. (1970). Bridge over troubled waters. On *Bridge over troubled waters* [Record]. United States: Columbia.

Stevenson, R. L. (1981). *Treasure Island* (Rev. ed.). New York: Scribner. (Original work published 1911)

Sturges, P. (1998). *Bridges are to cross.* New York: Putnam Books.

Swift, H., & Ward, L. (2002). *The little red lighthouse and the great gray bridge.* San Diego: Harcourt Press.

Wargin, K. (1998). *The legend of sleeping bear.* Chelsea, MI: Sleeping Bear Press.

Warner Brothers golden jubilee 24-karat collection Road Runner/Wile E. Coyote the classic chase. (1990). United States: Warner Brothers Home Video.

Weatherford, C. (2002). *Remember the bridge: Poems of a people.* New York: Philomel Books.

Winters, J. (2005). *Mystic Uncle and the magical bridge.* Coral Springs, FL: Llumina Press.

Index

CORWIN PRESS

The Corwin Press logo—a raven striding across an open book—represents the union of courage and learning. Corwin Press is committed to improving education for all learners by publishing books and other professional development resources for those serving the field of PreK–12 education. By providing practical, hands-on materials, Corwin Press continues to carry out the promise of its motto: **"Helping Educators Do Their Work Better."**